BLUESTOCKING

■ **Helen Fletcher** was a suffragist in the 1920s, was married and had two children in the 1930s, and did not begin her career as a writer until 1944, three years before she died at the age of 37. In those three years she established herself as film critic of *Time and Tide*, *Women's Own* and the *Daily Graphic*, and at the time of her death she had been commissioned to write a screen-play on the life of Lord Byron. Her unfinished autobiography – originally to have been entitled *A Gay Goodnight* – is presented here exactly as she left it, and with an Introduction by Dilys Powell. As an afterword we print an Introduction written by C.V. Wedgwood in 1947, before it was decided that the book was too near the bone for immediate publication.

BLUESTOCKING

Helen Fletcher

With an introduction by
Dilys Powell, 1985

And a letter of introduction by
C.V. Wedgwood, 1947

PANDORA

London, Boston and Henley

Never to have lived is best, ancient writers say;
Never to have drawn the breath of life, never to have
  looked into the eye of day;
The second best's a gay goodnight and quickly turn away.
From *Oedipus at Colonus*, W.B. Yeats

First published in 1986
by Pandora Press
(Routledge & Kegan Paul plc)

14 Leicester Square, London WC2H 7PH, England

9 Park Street, Boston, Mass. 02108, USA and

Broadway House, Newtown Road,
Henley on Thames, Oxon RG9 1EN, England

Set in Sabon 11/13 pt.
by Columns of Reading
and printed in Great Britain
by The Guernsey Press Co Ltd,
Guernsey, Channel Islands

Library of Congress Cataloging in Publication Data

Fletcher, Helen, d. 1947.

Bluestocking.
I. Title.
PR6011.L485B5 1986 791.43'092'4 [B] 85-21534
British Library CIP data also available

ISBN 0-86358-075-0 (c)
0-86358-071-8 (p)

– INTRODUCTION –

It must have been getting on for three years since I had read a book when Helen Fletcher's autobiography was put into my hands. For three years I had been ruled by necessity. I had read what I had to read: the newspaper, the cast lists and synopses of films, all the mass of relevant information which confronts the cinema critic. Cataract had inhibited the long slow exploration of a book, and the screen had to satisfy the craving for fiction. Now, after the operation which is one of today's miracles, I could read for pleasure, and by great good fortune my first experience was provided by Helen Fletcher's book.

It was the story of a life on which my own had touched. Helen was a film critic; she wrote for *Time and Tide*, she wrote for the *Sunday Graphic*. There were not many women in the game at the time. There was Caroline Lejeune, true creator of British cinema criticism. There was Arnot Robertson, a distinguished novelist who spoke about films on radio and was an early defender of critical independence. Helen herself used to talk about Elspeth Grant. Her own appearance in the company was a notable event. One was aware of a pleasing addition to the audience at press shows.

She was liked by her colleagues. I regret my failure to take advantage of the chance to know her. Especially I blame myself for a botched opportunity. In the years after the war British film critics were beginning to attend Continental festivals. There was a festival at Prague. It came early; liberation was still recent, and Czechoslovakia was understandably short of accommodation. When I arrived I was told I was to share a room with Helen Fletcher.

I knew I should have to send a report of the programmes back to the *Sunday Times*. The thought of writing it in a shared bedroom and of exposing to strange eyes the painful slowness at which I wrote filled me with alarm. I said I would sleep in a bathroom if necessary, but alone. I made a great fuss, and I was given a room to myself.

Probably Helen was as reluctant as I was. But my protest was extremely unpopular with those of the other critics who came to hear of it. I was not actually ostracised, but I was made to feel the disapproval. And I am still ashamed; even more ashamed now that I have read in this autobiography about the miseries inflicted by unwelcoming companions. I hope that Helen did not know of my shrinking. But I bet she did.

Her story is tragi-comic; the early life was dominated by a special kind of rejection. One would emphasise the tragic aspect were the record not illumined by a girl's resistance. Of course there is a rejection common to all outsiders at school. Children are creatures of convention. They gang up against the unusual arrival. Like birds, they mob the stranger with plumage unlike their own. And Helen was unusual. She was an oddity. She hated games. She liked poetry. She wore her alien psychological colours on her skin. They were immediately recognised, and her reception in the dormitory on her first evening at boarding school, though it is absurd, was painful. 'Shall we torture her?' asks one of the two occupants of the room. No doubt Helen exaggerates, but then she is a writer; she makes a good story of her wretchedness, especially of an accident which looked like suicide. The ironic observer is there in the account of the conversation as mistresses tried to bring her round: 'There must be no talking. Anyone who says a word will miss netball tomorrow.'

She was doubly unfortunate in her school. The unpopular boy, the girl who shuns athletic companions, sometimes finds solace in the sympathy of a teacher. Helen describes an establishment which had been warned against her; she was in favour with nobody. She was unsatisfactory material; but she would be re-shaped, mentally and physically. Helen insists that she was a plain girl. The image one recalls is of a lively, welcoming face, a smiler. Fashions in faces change, and she may not have conformed to the tastes of her day, but she can never have been plain. She was the victim of misjudgment: she was the ugly duckling and nobody recognised the lineaments of the swan. At the age of ten, already gifted, she was committed to an establishment devoted to turning out semi-literates for the marriage market.

The autobiography is thus a story of growing up against odds, and it is set against a hostile social background. Society weighted the odds against her; and family was on the side of society. One is inclined to think that today a daughter has as good a chance of a professional career as a son. One hears, though, of only the successes; doubt creeps in. Helen Fletcher was educated at a time when conditions were changing but had not yet affected the rooted convictions of the middle class. She could see a free world waiting for her; she was not to be allowed to enter it. Her mother believed that for a girl of her class the only life possible was marriage. To this end the child must be trained and educated. She must be formed to trap a man: what else was there for her to do? She must have the looks and the dress for the part. She must be prepared for the social occasions attendant on the role. Those were the days of the tennis-party, and proficiency in the mixed doubles was a mark of eligibility. A girl with prospects had curly hair and a good backhand.

The reluctant candidate would be repeatedly reminded of her lack of promise. One has forgotten the middle-class woman given to discussing the personal faults of a child in his presence. Helen was again and again reminded of the paucity of her chances and the improbability of her netting a husband. The story she tells is of relentless exposure to humiliation and the undermining of self-confidence. Her education seems to have been directed to crushing her gifts, to eradicating her imagination and driving her towards the conventional and the commonplace.

Many girls of her day would have been happy enough with her life. There was money in the family; she may have been reproved but she was scarcely neglected. She had toys, she had pets; you might say she was pampered. It was just that fate had placed a barrier between her nature and her circumstances. And with all her strength she drove herself towards her proper goal. She resisted. And from her resistance to misdirection this remarkable book was born.

Remarkable and mysterious.

The main body of the work as it stands holds the suggestion of tragedy: the gifted girl imprisoned in a life which denies her the exercise of her gifts. Presently light begins to filter into the tunnel. On a visit to her godmother in the Lake District she tastes a quiet freedom which she appreciates only in retrospect. She is sent – the decision was a relic of social customs long past – to finishing school in Paris. And here she is neither rejected by her companions nor reproved by the head of the establishment. A schoolgirl passion for a fellow-emigrée from boarding school is not reciprocated; but in general she seems to be all right. And then the record stops. No account of the transition to adult life, no description of the beginnings of a professional career, nothing. One can piece together some sort of outline from other sources, but the accents of personal experience are missing. Nearly twenty years of a life are missing.

Confounding the predictions of her mother, Helen Fletcher married. Her husband was a son of the Bishop of Salisbury. He was among the children encountered in her description of a visit to the flooded Cathedral; the pair, one gathers, were united by their feeling for the city and the neighbourhood. He became a schoolmaster at Westminster, a teacher of the classics, and there was a move to London. The marriage was finally broken, but without acrimony, by divorce, and during the war Helen settled with her children and a woman friend in a Dorset village. From the elder son, now an Oxford don, one has the impression of a contented life of journalism and writing.

Helen was doing well. She was the film critic of *Time and Tide* and the *Sunday Graphic*. Her work was sought after; Beaverbrook tried, but failed, to persuade her to break her agreement with the *Sunday Graphic* and write for him. Looking now at her film criticism one sees an easy popular style, very personal, very forthright. She likes Fred Astaire but can live without Bing Crosby, she deplores the prevalence of the violent, she wants more emphasis on everyday characters. 'Do they ever make films about you? They never make films about me.' The taste is impeccable; the style is nicely graded between *Time and Tide* and the *Sunday Graphic*, and in each case it is quite different from the direct and sometimes astringent manner of the autobiography – which one gathers she was engaged on at the time. Her career seemed to be set for major success.

Then – it was in 1947 – there was a telephone call to the ex-husband, with whom the two sons were staying. There had been a domestic accident: a fall. There was a fifty-fifty chance of recovery; but no. On the very threshold of achievement Helen Fletcher died. She was only thirty-seven.

Autobiography is confidently embarked on by the non-writer. Unpractised essays sometimes survive by virtue of their material. The Second World War, geographically wide-ranging, an exercise-ground for adventure and spectacular escapes, provided the narratives: autobiography almost took the place of fiction. Helen Fletcher had no adventures to describe. Her life was beginning. Her story was limited to the years of childhood and school, and a schoolgirl's story is notoriously uninviting to the normal reader. Yet from this slender and transparent stuff she created not only a personal record but a notable social picture. Of course the book is flawed. Sometimes it might be the expression of inexperience; had she lived she would have revised. But always there is the sense of the immediate. It is as if the incidents of childhood and adolescence had affected her only yesterday. Sometimes it might be the child, the girl herself writing.

The personal story develops into an indictment of a section of a social class. And the personal story itself is full of struggle. The child at the start is deeply religious; the loss of the belief and the resolute self-discipline of breaking away from it are tackled as if the narrative presented no problem. Helen carries on as if she did not notice the problem. Many professional writers would have paused nervously before the struggle to present the character of the mother whose resolute misdirection ruled the early life of her daughter. The struggle does not show; the character emerges naturally from behaviour and conversation: it is simply there. The figure of the writer herself is drawn with an engaging mixture of the frank and the ironic. The writer never seems to draw back to look at herself. One sees a young creature, gnawed by ambitions and desires, but pitiless in the midst of her own unhappiness.

The writing is simple, undecorated, at its best when the author is trapped in the prison of upbringing and education and her own resentments. There is a passage, a paragraph, no more, about the death of her dog; nobody could have done it better. Yet she can lose her aassurance when the affairs of the adult world impinge. Incautiously allowed to spend the day with a young officer friend of the family and given a discreet view of the love-nest he visits, though looking back after two decades she recognises the situation she does not bring it to the edge one finds elsewhere. At the last we see her, free from family, in the semi-sophisticated setting of the finishing school, and here, though the visual observation is sharp enough, the critical personal reaction is replaced by convention.

Had she lost her subject? She had covered what to most writers would have been the most elusive chapters, the farthest removed. One wonders whether the more dangerous revelations of adult life, its uncomfortable complications, had deterred her. A curious quality in the writing, too, is mysterious. It isn't the work of the innocent eye – or if it is the eye is uncommonly knowing, not the kind of eye the unwary adult wants to have about the place. It doesn't merely record behaviour and incidents, it notes relationships, it picks up the secret signals which pass between characters who meet and talk and are not aware of signalling. Even as a child Helen Fletcher knew what the people around her were up to.

And yet in the midst of these evidences of perception she will find time to chronicle some detail, trivial and meaningless, of a child's life. When she comes to describe her days in Paris the disturbing insight has vanished. She observes, but the observation is superficial. She puts her own interpretation on social obstruction and on the family which subscribed to it. She has not learned, or at any rate does not show that she has learned, to put her own interpretation on an alien adult world.

The anomaly, then, persists between the critical observer and the simple record of experience long ago. Helen Fletcher writes as two people. Sometimes it is as if she were the child who, growing into adolescence, puts down on paper her immediate sensations. Sometimes she is the woman looking back with the analytical judgment of maturity. Sometimes the two writers combine, and then we see an extraordinary picture of what it was like to be an unhappy, questioning child. It is a rare exploration of one of the fastnesses of life. It is to be cherished.

Dilys Powell

– 1 –

When I was six I knew I was Jesus' sister. Standing high on my seat in the box pew, I read out loudly and slowly those portions of the Morning Prayer prescribed for the Vicar only. When he cursed I cursed, when he blessed I blessed. Firmly and passionately I implored God in the Litany to have mercy on all men, but especially on women labouring of child. This last was too much for my father.

'Take her out, Nurse, take her out.'

I was led out ignominiously, still praying. It was a pity because I had looked forward to giving the congregation my blessing. I felt they would be the better for it, and that God had relied on me to do it. I had let God down. I sat down on a tombstone, and listened while Nannie told me what the Fawcett's Nannie would think of her. Gradually her voice swamped the voice of God.

At tea-time the Vicar came himself. It was difficult for him, I know now, because my parents paid for his summer holiday. Offending them might mean the loss of a fortnight with his wife at the Grosvenor Hotel, Swanage. Nevertheless, he put his cloth first. Patiently and tolerantly, he explained the difference between versicle and response. The congregation said one, the Vicar the other. It was, he knew, difficult for a little girl. A pity, in some ways, that I tried to read so soon, before I could understand the words. It was, my mother agreed, a pity. She had never thought to rear a child who was such a bluestocking. Now you never saw my brother without a ball.

Perhaps, the Vicar suggested, I would be better at the Children's Service. I would understand the words better, and they would be more suitable. I did, and they were, but the poetry was gone. Lacking the Litany, I murmured anaemically of Gentle Jesus, while my brother ate up blackberries. It was Harvest Festival; no one rebuked him. The flowers on the Altar, the peaches on the window sills, the giant and inedible marrows round the lectern, all were ours. The Vicar used a different voice when he spoke to us from the one he used for the village children, and he spoke to God in a different voice. Where last Sunday there had been power and majesty, now there was gentleness and facetiousness. It was not Mr Cook's fault he was not George Herbert. He was a good man and a fine scholar, and if he never said a serious word to children he obeyed the custom of his period. I realised that if God and I knew that the world was tragic and majestic, no one else knew it; or if they did to show it would have been what my mother called Bad Form. My brother and visiting children could repeat Adam and Eve and Pinch-me unendingly, but if I was heard muttering, 'O Lamb of God that takest away the sins of the world' I was shaken and told: 'We don't want any more of *that*.'

I was not a pretty or an easy child. My mother preferred my brother, and rightly. Looking back on those nursery days of 1914-16, I realise that my only personal relationship was with God. Even now when I no longer believe in Him, the Lord of Hosts is no abstraction to me, but someone with whom I once shared petits beurres. I do not remember ever knowing, at that time, anyone who was deeply religious. My parents were Church of England by class and convention, believing easily but not caring deeply. I remember that it seemed incredible to me then that anyone should believe and not care. It seems so still. As an atheist I have more sympathy for the man who chains himself to a rock and starves himself to death for the Kingdom of Heaven than for those jaunty Christians who believe God will pardon us if we do our best. At six I could not make much of Christ's birth, being ignorant of the facts of life, but I understood his death very well. Like the man in the cave I longed to suffer with him. I was too carefully watched to secrete whips or chains, so I thought of a subtler plan. For days I eschewed the lavatory. Nannie replied with purgatives. Still I eschewed the lavatory. It was not, I knew, appropriate, but it hurt, and I offered the pain to God in hopeless atonement for my mother's Sunday tennis teas, my father's billiards, the servants' young men and all the worldliness of our house.

Red House, Park Lane, Salisbury was, I can see now, no villa in Gomorrah, though 1914-16 found it as it found most of the homes of the English middle classes, smug and sleek and fat. My father and my mother and my friends' fathers and mothers had discovered with a bump that they were mortal. To eat, drink and be merry was pagan beyond their capacity, but within the limit of the Salisbury ethic they pursued the good time. Or rather my mother pursued it. My father went on with his work, bicycling to the office instead of driving, guarding Salisbury tunnel every alternative Tuesday, reading the casualties before the cricket scores in *The Times* – a gentleman for whom the moderate was the right. Like the Roman soldier who stood at attention while lava drowned him, my father knew no alternative to good behaviour. Sometimes at parties when a good deal of alcohol has reduced my contemporaries to the condition that our generation calls natural, and they lie about the floor tormented by inhibitions no longer, I go upstairs to powder my nose and see my father's face in the glass.

I thought in childhood that it was a cold face. I see now that it was a controlled one. My father felt the same emotions as other people, but he did not feel that the world wished to be told them. Once at Christmas I accepted a third helping of plum pudding, saying that I adored it.

'No,' said my father, 'you adore none save God.'

He was wrong. I adored God and plum pudding. He adored nothing and neither. He *liked* a plantain-free tennis lawn, the clink of billiards balls, bridge with the doctors on Tuesdays. Although he was a games-fiend, my father was socially circumspect: *good bridge was played with doctors, good* golf with clergymen and solicitors. Professionalism in sport was abominable to him. I remember how gently and carefully he explained the etiquette of the Golf Club to my six-year-old brother for whom the professional had made a miniature bag of clubs.

'Mr Clegg is a nice man who makes clubs and is paid to play golf with us. We do not shake hands with him. Mr Carruthers does not make clubs and is not paid to play golf. We do.'

Mr Carruthers was the Club Secretary.

'Anyhow,' said Ronald, 'Mr Clegg plays better.'

‘That,’ said my father, ‘is beside the point.’

But I think he wished it were not. Mr Carruthers drank and bought with kisses Kummels from the wives of members, and as was to be expected his golf suffered. The professional did not drink and lived as one dedicated. I believe that for once my father doubted the wisdom of class.

My mother never doubted it. The war offered her opportunities for condescension beyond her wildest dreams. Our house was near enough to the aerodrome and camp to be a free hotel for soldiers. We learnt tennis with lieutenants, dancing with captains, and finally after being bathed by Nannie's sergeant, smuggled up the back stairs, said our prayers to an American general, confident that if ‘Please God give me a bicycle’ did not produce one by the morning, our charm would indeed have failed.

In justice to my religious feelings, I must own that this ruse was my brother's, and that after the grown-ups had gone down to dinner, I climbed out of bed and offered my apologies to God, removing the nursery rug and kneeling remorsefully on cold linoleum.

‘Whatever happens, we must be brave for the sake of the children,’ my mother would declare courageously, dabbing her eyes with a lace handkerchief, when any visitor tactlessly mentioned a major defeat of the war.

‘Poor little dears,’ said Cook, ‘they didn't ask to be born.’

We were, we realised, creatures of some pathos, and we played our parts heroically if self-consciously. Arrayed as a Red Cross nurse and British Tommy respectively, we gave ginger beer to all troops within reach. Fifty wounded Tommies came to eat strawberries and cream on the lawn and play Nuts and May at our birthday parties.

'So wonderful of you, Mrs Fletcher – such patriotism!'

'Not at all, matron. I just feel I must do my little bit!'

At Christmas my brother and I gave tea to a ward in the infirmary.

'Will you have a cigarette or a banana, soldier?' we were told to ask at each bed, shaking hands gravely with such patients as retained a hand. I was terrified, imagining too well the stench beneath the Lysol, the wounds beneath the carefully folded bedclothes. Everywhere there were balloons and crackers, even the bedpans were decorated rather incongruously with holly. Somehow the decoration made it worse. I feared that some man not wanting a banana or a packet of Players would tell me to go away in a rude voice.

It says a lot for the patience of the Tommies that none ever did. Instead, they said, 'Thank you kindly, Missie,' or 'Isn't she a fine girl, Sister?' and in less than no time I was back again on the platform where Mummy was preparing to sing *Danny Boy* and Ronald was telling the house surgeon about the football in his stocking.

Danny Boy was the theme song of my childhood. My mother had what is called a fine drawing-room contralto; what she lacked in music she made up in sentiment. On Sunday afternoons, after a rich lunch, the only one of the week eaten away from Nannie and in the dining-room, we perched ourselves on the sides of the fender, and our parents made music. Neither played the piano, and to this end they imported Mr Russell Davies, the first distinguished person I ever knew. He was small and fat, and had hands like a woman's and he lived in a small damp house (Queen Anne, I know now) with an island in his garden and a bridge to walk across to it. He kept a man-servant called George, who stole the silver every month and fled to Bournemouth, only to be caught and brought back by the police. Far from feeling indignant or angry, Mr Davies behaved as though this was the most natural occurrence in the world. My mother, however, was indignant for him. 'Such base ingratitude,' she would say to Mrs Fawcett, and Mrs Fawcett would answer proudly, '*My* husband says he should be horsewhipped when he's brought back, and what does his master do but welcome him, kiss him even.' Looking back, I wonder if she were not more accurate than she knew. Anyhow, George continued his monthly disappearances and Mr Davies continued to live in a house so damp that the keys of his Bechstein stuck when he played his favourite Chopin.

It is amusing to notice that whereas I can remember much that Salisbury said of Mr Davies, I remember nothing that he said of Salisbury. Why, for instance, did he come to our house every Sunday? Was it perhaps the lunch? Was George a poor cook as well as a thief? Was Mr Davies in fact not rich as people said – he did not work and disdained to publish the children's stories he wrote for us, the best I ever remember – but so poor that good food cancelled bad conversation? Often between the songs his fingers would find other tunes on our carefully tended Broadwood pianola.

'What's that you are playing, Russell?' my mother would ask jealously.

'Nothing, dear Kitty, an old tune. Weren't you going to sing *Because*?'

Only once do I remember him smiling at us, instead of with us. My mother was singing her favourite. It was called *Jeunesse*, and it said:

I have taken your picture out of its frame,
And out of my prayers I have taken your name,
I have crumpled your letters into the flame,
And yet in my heart you are there just the same.
Does the Bon Dieu I wonder, commend me
or blame?

At the word 'flame' her voice broke, she sought her lace handkerchief. 'It's no good, Russell. I can't bear that today. It's too like life.'

She swept from the room.

'Well, Davies,' said my father, 'how about *Trumpeter*? That should put some guts back into us!'

'Of course – but your wife. . . .'

'She'll be all right,' said my father grimly. 'Enjoying yourselves, children?'

I spoke truly when I said we were. I knew my mother was pretending. I was glad no one went after her. I knew I hated her. As for my brother, he was always happy in the drawing-room.

My father barked his way through *Trumpeter* and dallied deliciously between *Friend o' Mine* and *The Company Sergeant Major*.

'Now,' said Mr Davies, with unusual firmness, '*Pleading*.'

I put on my religious face. *Pleading*, I know now, is by Elgar. I knew then only that it made me feel like church before Mr Cook had spoilt it.

Will you come homeward from the hills of dreamland?
I have grown weary though I wait you yet,
Watching the fallen leaf, the faith grown fainter,
The memory smoulder to a dim regret.

I am at a loss to say now whether the words have

any value, and yet when my father's voice sang:

> Quicken my hope and recompense my pain

I had that feeling in the tummy that only comes for art. I had no notion what the words meant, but I felt I knew if not Good from Evil at least True from False, and that I had a place of my own at last, and the place was in Mr Davies' world and not in my mother's.

– 2 –

Childhood, psychologists admit now, is rarely a happy time. I am grateful to them for admitting it and for destroying with one blow the tyranny of Peter Pan.

I do not want to grow old, I abominate each fresh wrinkle, eyeing forty with horror and fifty with dread, nevertheless I can contemplate seventy to eighty with more philosophy than I could re-live seven to eight.

'The best years of their lives,' my mother would say to Nannie. 'It makes one happy to watch them, nothing to worry about, no social duties, no need to think where the next penny's to come from, nothing to do but play!'

My brother and I would build our card-houses self-consciously, trying to look as radiant as her rhetoric inferred. We played prettily enough, certainly, but what my mother failed to realise was that playing hurt. I felt virtuous and happy putting my one-legged bear to bed, but when the next day I forgot to get him up I was stricken with remorse. I was treacherous, a failure. I played Ludo and promised myself, 'It will be all right if yellow wins,' but red won, and I was exposed once more to the implacable vengeance of my gods.

They were gentle enough in the daytime, these deities, gentle that is if you propitiated them, but at night! Shall I ever forget that feeling as darkness fell?

We would be in the drawing-room playing Hunt the Thimble. It was a long narrow room with grey carpets and pink chintzes; no shadows only flowers and the amiability of firelight. There would be a knock at the door, Nannie would be waiting for us.

'I'll be up in a few minutes to say goodnight,' Mummy would promise, disappearing at once into that magic world which claims all adults when children go to bed. Then would come the delights of our shared bath: toy boats, lost soap and the final and forbidden rainbow slide. But always the horror drew nearer. We slept in the night nursery together. It had white walls and rugs and an aeroplane frieze designed especially for us by a London artist. Secretly we disliked it very much but we knew it was smart and we lacked the integrity to speak up.

Beneath a parade of 1916 bombers Mummy would hear our prayers: 'God bless Mummy and Daddy and all our kind friends and all the soldiers, sailors and airmen and make me a good girl.' Here followed a private soliloquy intended theoretically for God only. Finally, and rather sleepily:

'Gentle Jesus, meek and mild,
Look upon a little child;
Pity my simplicity,
Suffer me to come to Thee.

Fain I would to Thee be brought;
Dearest God, forbid it not;
In the Kingdom of Thy Grace,
Grant a little child a place.'

'But what does it mean, pity mice?' Ronald would ask. The explanation would be drowned in kisses and exclamations to Nannie about the innocence of Mummy's angel.

'But I don't understand about "Fain I would," ' I asked seriously.

Neither I imagine did my mother, but she did not want to say so in front of Nannie.

'It means let me come to you when I die but do not let me die tonight. Goodnight, my darlings, Mummy must dress.'

'Nannie! Nannie!' I shrieked when she had put out the light. 'Nannie, I want you quickly!'

'What is it, my love? You know you mustn't call after Mummy's said goodnight. Do you want a drink of water?'

'Nannie, do people die in bed?'

'Bless me, of course not! What a question!'

'But Mummy said they did. What did she mean?'

'Well perhaps they do just fall asleep and not wake up. It's a good way to go. But you don't want to think about that now. Think about your new teddy. . . .'

'Oh God,' I prayed when she had gone, 'don't take me tonight, don't let death come. Let me be alive tomorrow. I'll be so good. Oh God, if you let me wake up I won't hit Ronald and I'll feed all the animals, and I'll love Mummy as much as Daddy.'

Gradually the darkness possessed the night nursery.

'Are you awake, Ronald?' 'Yes, are you – Yes – Goodnight, Goodnight.'

But soon there was no answer. He was asleep.

I heard Nannie gather up her sewing and go down to the kitchen for supper.

The night-light seemed to flicker. I could hear the nursery clock tick. If it stopped I should be dead. People always died when clocks stopped. There was a song about it:

> Stopped short, never to go again
> Now the old man's died.

I had thought it funny when Cook sang it. If the clock stops I shall die. If the night-light goes out it will mean the Dark Angel has come for me. The window curtain swung out:

'Oh God!' I screamed, 'Not yet! Not yet!'

My mother rushed into the room in her petticoat, disturbed in the middle of dressing.

'What is this absurd noise? I thought your brother had a nightmare.'

She shook me angrily.

'I expect she dreamed, Mum, she does sometimes.'

Nannie had returned to defend me, her mouth full of kitchen kipper.

'Nonsense, Nurse, the boy dreams, with the girl it's affectation. She must learn to control herself. Go back to your supper.'

It was true Ronald dreamed, but how happily he contrived it, waking in the middle of dinner parties to run downstairs barefoot, pink-cheeked and tousled and precipitate himself into his adoring mother's arms.

'Of course, poor angel, he can't help it,' she would tell the visitors. 'You know Sir William Bragg, the Harley Street nerve man, well, Stephen had him down. It cost a fortune of course. He said there was nothing we could do about it. Only love him and understand.'

Then all the ladies would make noises of extreme tenderness and solicitude and the gentlemen would felicitate my father:

'By Jove, Fletcher, you're a lucky chap! I doubt if there is any sight so pretty as a charming woman with her son in her arms!'

In the morning before Nannie woke we would share the booty of crystallised fruit that Ronald had hidden in his pyjama pocket to save for me.

He was always generous and loyal with the disarming sweetness of spoilt princes.

'Look, I saved this specially for you!' he would whisper, proffering a much slept-on greengage.

'What,' I would ask impatiently, 'are we going to do today?'

'Oh, just have fun. Are you liking your special fruit?'

Dear Ronald, the world has dealt as cruelly with him as it deals with all spoilt princelings. Girls who won't be kissed, cars that won't be sold, jobs that influence cannot hold, separate him from the boy I once knew; only so strong is the child in man that on those days when the Bank Manager mars his breakfast with his peculiarly caddish invective nothing can ever mar Ronald's conviction that the day will be fun.

Perhaps, after all, psychologists are wrong to inveigh so bitterly against Mother Fixation. The world is so full of duteous Nordic he-men proclaiming with every breath that life for them is real and earnest, surely it can support a few lounge lizards to lean on the bonnets of 1929 Bentleys in Great Portland Street and assure each other in cosy bars round Piccadilly that everything will be grand tomorrow, grandfather must die sometime, Flopsy's a wonderful greyhound, and anyway there is always the Irish Sweep.

Now when I pick up the telephone and hear Ronald's voice demanding 'Am I free today-he-is-in-the-Hell-of-a-jam-I-say-couldn't-we-go-to-the-flick-' I pick up my cheque book and muse on the difference which twenty-five years ago made me child of darkness and him a child of light.

Certainly it had something to do with catching balls. If someone threw one he caught it and I missed it. On this seemingly insignificant small detail hung the weight of my inadequacy and failure. How I hated balls, how I still hate them! I never see a goal scored in British Movietone News or watch the doctor's daughter reach her racquet up daintily and accurately without remembering my shame and their tyranny.

Tennis, cricket, golf, football, billiards, for Ronald every ball was magical, a spell to change a small boy into a god. Whether it was the gardener who crept in for a clandestine game of billiards, or the general who wanted an audience for his googlies, all male adults worshipped Ronald. He was the sort of son they longed for, or the sort of boy they knew they had been before an unfair world had sullied them.

He held himself well, he said Sir, he was modest, he did not cry unduly; at five he pressed his shorts under the cot mattress. He never asked questions that were difficult for grown-ups to answer, he was not intense.

As for me: with alien adult eyes I look back on an ungainly girl whose nose ran, who could not tie up her shoes, who thought too much of death and loved God and a Labrador retriever more than her mother.

'Of course she should have been the boy,' visitors said. 'She's more the build.'

I knew they meant it would not matter so much if the boy were plain.

'A dear girl, of course,' they always added kindly, 'but not *you* exactly. Who is she like?'

How well I knew the answer! Molly, my husband's only sister. Molly who likes books more than hats, who has been to Oxford to one of those dowdy women's colleges, who does not *want* to get married.

My mother kept a special inflection for that 'want'. No one was kinder than she to the local unmarriageables, to the doctor's daughter with such-pretty-hair-but-what-a-voice-dear; to Babs Howes who came to us for long hopeful visits and pursued the young officers with deathly flippancy.

'What, reading again!' Babs accosted me one day. 'Don't you know men hate clever women. Better run out and play or you'll grow up a bluestocking and no one will marry you.'

I longed to tell her, 'You couldn't be clever even if men liked it and even though you're stupid they don't marry you,' but I knew I must not commit the unspeakable error of 'answering' grown-ups. This came high in Nannie's crime list, second only to 'kicking-your-poor-little-brother-where-it-might-injure-him-for-life-and-you-know-what-that-means!'

Instead I looked at her innocently and said: 'Will you come here next year and the year after forever and ever? I mean if you *don't* get married?'

To return to Aunt Molly. Aunt Molly was clever, men did not like Aunt Molly, Aunt Molly did not mind men not liking her. To go back to my mother's inflection, she did not even *want* to get married.

'My dear, you'll never believe it, when Helen was a wee babe, Molly brought one of her extraordinary friends to stay. Well, one day they were watching me bath the baby, and I said, you know, feeling sorry for them, "Don't you wish she was yours, Molly?" and what do you think, the friend turned round and snapped my head off – "Molly", she said, "has more important things to think of than bathing babies!" '

One week-day evening when we came down to the

drawing-room my father was there as well as my mother. He had come back from the office early bringing a sheaf of bills. £200 to Marshall and Snelgroves, £60 to Bradleys, £40 to the local Arts and Crafts. My mother was all that people mean when they say senselessly extravagant, they might justly have added tastelessly. Flowers, fur coats, new curtains and silk dresses were human and happy but who could forgive her those barbola waste paper baskets and mirrors with Pan playing a dreary little tune when you powdered your nose? My father was tolerant and fair and patient. I do not think he minded much about possessions. It was all the same to him if she wasted his substance on Poole pottery or Crown Derby, but he feared the consequence of such wasted substance. The son of temperate North Country gentry who had been rich for three hundred years, he could not tolerate waste of money. Looking back I can feel sorry for my mother without in any way condoning the barbola. Her extravagance was the warmest thing about her. My brother and I had no notion of the reason for the strife which pervaded the drawing-room but we felt it was there and we settled down on the hearth-rug to build card-houses fervently if unobtrusively.

Hearth-rugs are a shocking site for building especially when they are ruckled by angry parental feet, nevertheless we built manfully. Ronald achieved a tower, inadvertantly I jolted it, and it fell. He screamed and hit me, I wept. Intervening abruptly, my mother slapped my face. She never hit us but today the bills had unnerved her.

My father picked me up and wiped my face on his office handkerchief:

'Really, Kitty, you are grossly unfair. I do not like to

see favouritism.'

'Of course I favour the boy – he's the love of my life and just like me. Helen grows more like your family every day. She's cold and unfeeling and awkward – mark my words she'll grow up the image of your sister Molly.'

My father put me down and rang the bell.

'Take the children up to their Nurse,' he told the parlourmaid. 'Tell her I will come up later to say goodnight to them.'

At the top of the stairs Winifred had a great deal to whisper to Nannie.

'Mark my works – it won't last long. You should have seen the Master's face and the Mistress was crying. . . .'

'Hush,' Nannie said. She closed the nursery baize door with the air of a Bishop extending sanctuary. 'There'll be half an hour before your bath. Nannie and Bertha will help you with your transfers.' Then seeing our tear-stained faces, 'There my poor angels, Nannie'll look after her babies.'

Always when I hear husbands and wives who hate each other declare that they will stay together 'for the sake of the children' I remember Nannie's face as she closed that baize door.

'Of course,' my mother tells me when we meet now, 'I was not like you at your age. I did not think of jobs and parties. My life was dedicated. Ah well, things are different now, but at least I have the satisfaction of knowing I was a perfect mother.'

It is a satisfaction I shall never know. Probably in 1960 my sons will be writing books about how I misunderstood them. Only whatever they remember it won't be 'a darkness on the stair' and they will have known a household where love is.

But Mr Russell Davies and Nannie were not my only allies. Reeves, our gardener, himself the father of twelve, was my dear friend and staunch defender. When with horrid regularity, on the first Wednesday in the month, Monsieur Blanchette the local hairdresser mounted his bicycle and peddled up the hill to singe my hair it was Reeves who allowed me to hide in the potting shed or asparagus bed. I cannot imagine why I minded Monsieur Blanchette singeing my hair, which was long and straight and apparently needed it, but the sight of the bicycle with the little black bag on the back of it propped against our railings filled me with terror.

I can well remember lying lost in asparagus fern holding my breath while Mummy and Nannie searched the garden.

'There, you're all safe now – Reeves' pretty,' the old man would comfort me. 'Be a good girl, little Missie, and Reeves'll tell you his poetry.'

And I would lie still lulled in peace in my green bed while his old Wiltshire voice told of a little girl whose plight was far worse than mine.

I have never read Tennyson's *May Queen* since for fear that adult good taste might come between me and the memory of that kitchen garden sanctuary.

I loved Reeves so much that I longed to talk like him. Ronald and I would contrive to interpolate as many of his phrases as possible into our conversation. The one I can remember now is 'I can't h'abide a h'egg', and of course there was the inevitable 'Eh.' 'But who teaches you to say that?' amazed grown-ups would ask.

'We say it because Reeves says it and we love Reeves and want to be like him.'

Class distinction comes hard to children. All the

people they love are ineligible as friends and all the eligible friends are impossible to love. There was Charlie, Winifred's brother, who cleaned our shoes and helped Reeves in the garden. I loved Charlie. He had red hair and freckles and the wrong ears. Best of all he had a goat, a pompous and bearded Billie. I adored that goat which I met by appointment in the village. When I had measles I cried so much for it that by doctor's orders it was imported into the night nursery and stood very proud and sullen eyeing me from the bottom of the bed. I hope goats are impregnable to measles. Alas, the white rabbit I also had imported died from a surfeit of washing by Nannie who thought stuffed animals better adapted to sick beds.

I loved animals wildly, selfishly and inordinately. Selfishly because I wanted them always to be with me and to need me. I would not allow my rabbits privacy to breed their young or my guinea pigs privacy to eat their food. Consequently the inevitable tragedies occurred. Finding me spent with grief beside their furry corpses, Reeves would reason with me:

'Leave them be, Missie, try to leave them be.'

It was useless, I couldn't and I knew I couldn't. They perished from excess of my love as I longed to perish from excess of my tears.

'Well, which is it now?' my mother would inquire, finding me sobbing behind the drawing-room sofa where I confidently expected to perish undisturbed. As my menagerie included a Labrador retriever, a Belgian hare, two doves, six to twenty rabbits, eight to eighteen mice, numerous guinea pigs, two lovebirds, a goldfish and a tortoise, it was inevitable that something had proved mortal. Looking back it seems that my mother's patience in the matter of pets was extraordinary. If

Nannie had had her way she would have drowned the whole lot in the Avon.

'Well, thank goodness tomorrow's Tuesday,' my mother would say. 'Nannie must take you to the Market again.' And I would run off to arrange with Ronald about the funeral trying not to let my mind play too faithlessly with pictures of the new beast I would buy tomorrow.

It was my firm belief that one day I should own a white elephant. No adult scorn could ever dissuade me and even now when I see White Elephant Sale written up I feel a twinge of sadness for the mythical creature which was to have been the dearest pet of all.

Monkeys were always an inflexible taboo. In the words of Nannie, 'They had things.' But every other living thing lived with us and we seldom met my mother at the station unless she had a box marked Harrods, with holes for air bored in it, and through the holes just visible anonymous glinting eyes.

How odd it is, this passion for animals. I am an adult now and supposedly fulfilled in my children, and yet I never see a pet shop without stopping to look in the window, or glimpse a Great Dane across the road without a leaping heart.

As to my human relationships, class as I say corroded them. We played with the village gentry children, three in number and the wrong age, and with various Salisbury families which our parents selected or whose parents selected us. No one I remember ever asked us if we liked the selection. You could not choose children as you chose animals who are happily above and beyond the barriers of class.

My mother's chief friend was Mrs Rutland – a rich proud woman whose husband owned a saw-mill and tumbled one appalling morning into his fatally competent machinery.

My father, hearing of this, telephoned my mother to go and break the news to Mrs Rutland. We were not supposed to know but by the time she left on her errand of mercy in a hired Victoria – the car having been lent patriotically to a local doctor for the war period – the whole household was in a twitter and we were too excited to swallow the chicken broth which we had in winter for elevenses.

In an hour my mother was back, radiant in tears and furs.

'Well, Mum, how did the poor lady take it?' Nannie asked.

'Without a tear, Nurse, without a tear. I may be a weak woman but if it had been my Stephen. . . ah, well no one could call me hard.'

After this I was fond of Mrs Rutland. Secretly I admired her for not crying in front of Mummy and pitied her less for her husband's decease (now rumoured by the Close to be suicide, Heaven save me from the charity of Christians!) than for her children. Hermione, a year my senior, was an idiot even by Salisbury standards. Harold was Ronald's age and whiny and puny. They had two Norland nurses who starved them according to Nannie. Certainly when Harold stayed with us he was delighted to be given a whole egg. He slept in Daddy's dressing-room and when Daddy went in for a clean shirt called out: 'Don't come in yet, Mr Fletcher, you'll see my person.'

My brother and I, who ran races naked under the tennis lawn sprinkler and always bathed together till I was twelve, thought this behaviour very odd indeed.

Mrs Rutland did not approve of inter-class relationships (as if Harold would have had the guts to have any!) and to avoid them she had a special Wolf Cub pack formed for Harold, Ronald and five or six other suitable boys. Hermione, it was planned, should share our governess. My parents were speechless and troubled but they need not have worried. She only came once and sat and slobbered. During break in the garden she cried when the Labrador retriever licked her. The governess ran to comfort her, and I saw that Reeves had stopped mowing and was crying. After that she never came to see us and gradually drifted into a 'home'.

It was odd, my Mother said, that there were so many children like Hermione in Salisbury families, she meant in 'good' Salisbury families. I remember obscurely the girl of twenty at the Vicarage who would always be Mummy's baby and sat playing with dolls obscenely, and the doctor's son who grew younger not older at his birthdays, which were always celebrated by conjurers and magic lantern shows. A grim comment on provincial society!

But not all our contemporaries were idiots, though many were unconscionably dull.

Blood compelled us to play often with our cousins who lived in a William Morris house, went to church on Saints' Days and (intolerable offence) put prunes in their fruit salad at parties. There were eight of them and their mother died of a complaint I knew only as Nagony.

It was in fact cancer of the throat. My brother and I overheard a great deal about her suffering and the 'eight poor motherless darlings' she left behind her. but when we met them again it surprised us to find we disliked them none the less. The girls wore dark green dresses with collars and cuffs cut out of a mixture of dough and cardboard, or so one imagined. The boys wore shorts that were too long for them. All worked earnestly with needles and threads and fretsaws and when they needed relaxation played pencil and paper games. As I grew older I grew to dread the special one which demanded a morbidly intimate knowledge of Dickens, Whittier and Longfellow. 'It's funny isn't it,' Martha would say, 'that Helen never wins though she's meant to be so literary.'

Once a year these cousins gave a play at the Church Hall. It was always the same play. Martha and Mary, the two eldest, would lean out of a rather ricketty window and wave to the rest of the family who processed up the aisle singing *Onward Christian Soldiers* and inviting the audience to join them.

'Please Mummy let us go. . . please, please Mummy!' we would clamour excitedly.

'Certainly not!' said my mother. 'It's most vulgar. Give them a Mackintosh's toffee, Nannie.'

I do not think I wanted to be dressed like my cousins, but I know I longed to be as serious as they were.

The other day I met the youngest of them at a garden party and when he had fought for tea for me he told me that he and his brothers and sisters had been brought up to think my mother the Scarlet Woman and had collected news of Ronald's and my escapades since we grew up as other families collect news of film-stars.

'What are you doing now, Cousin Helen?' he asked wistfully.

I was loath to tell him I was living in the country with my children and longed to add that I had a black lover and smoked opium on Sundays.

One last reminiscence, this time against myself and so disgraceful that twenty years can scarcely dim the shame of it. My cousins, having fasted embarrassingly throughout Lent, embarrassingly because we never remembered, so always seemed to be tempting them, decided to have a children's party at Easter. We had parties often but this was special because it was not to begin till 5.30 and was to go on till 9 p.m. No one was invited under nine, I was asked and not my brother.

I shall never forget what I went through to get to that party. My father said I should go, it would be good for Ronald. My mother said I shouldn't, it would be bad for Ronald. Nannie, always sentimental, thought it a pity we should be separated, and rude of the cousins' Nannie.

I stormed, I begged, I wept, I threatened Ronald and appealed to Daddy; I sat sullen while my mother lectured me on selfishness. Finally she gave in. A blue chiffon frock was ordered instead of the white muslin which did for the dancing class and blue knickers to match with frills on them in case I fell over or pirouetted.

'Can you imagine, Nannie, her cousins wear cambric for parties and red flannelette in the day time?'

Also a new pair of bronze dancing sandals and a pocket handkerchief with lace on it.

'But what,' I asked, 'shall I wear to go in?'

'Why, your coat of course.'

'But Doreen has a white fur cape. I want one.'

Doreen was the daughter of the biggest local chemist who in spite of strong local feeling still came to the dancing classes.

'That is precisely why you shall not have one.'

Sadly I relegated the fur cape to dreamland along

with the prospect of being photographed not in jerseys as we were but naked except for blue tulle. The photographer's window was full of little girls clad like this and I could never understand my mother's disdain for the practice. Why were all common things so much nicer?

The night of the party found me sitting in a cab with Nannie and clutching my new handkerchief with (to make up for the fur cape) two drops of 4711 on it. Holding it to my nose I felt a vamp. Nannie abandoned me at the front door which was opened not by the usual shabby maid but by a borrowed butler. Upstairs in the spare room a strange maid took my coat. Clutching my scented handkerchief I slithered down the polished oak staircase trying hard to hold both shoulders level (Mummy said I dropped one) and to look and feel a lady.

A great many glass doors had been opened – what had once been hall and held golf clubs and hatstands was now part of a vast slippery ballroom.

My uncle, very strange in antique tails. Martha in blue satin with tulle in all possible decolletées stood in the middle of a sea of parquet.

'Name please – ' said the butler.

I was a girl alone on the staircase of a strange house. I was a girl in a blue dress who belonged to no one. I stood alone in time and unique in space. I had no name.

I sent my mind to find my voice and make it say Helen. Instead it found my bowels. A trumpet of wind escaped them. I had committed the blackest crime of all. I had done what Nannie most despised. At the first big party of my life I had made a fart and become a pariah.

Ignoring the borrowed butler I raced up the stairs and hid in the lavatory, to be rescued in two hours by the kind cook who smuggled me out of the back door to the waiting cab.

The pomp and glory of this world were not for me. Listening to the clip clop of the horse's hoofs I dedicated my life to the Mission Field.

– 3 –

No one ever asked me about the party. It was as if it had never been. I shut its memory in the back of my mind in the den where the monsters lived. Only when I was alone in bed or in the lavatory it slithered out to mock me. How terrible is the tyranny of the monsters at the back of the mind! Twenty years later I told my psychoanalyst the story of the party and I could not believe it when she laughed. She was a sane and sympathetic person yet an episode that had tortured me for years seemed funny to her. I almost kissed the butler I went away so shriven. Certainly the opponents of Freudian analysis cannot have made farts at children's parties.

About this time I met a real monster. I had always known I was afraid, now I knew what I was afraid of.

My brother and I walked with mother round the battlements of Old Sarum. It was an especially pleasant walk because of the Royalist secret passage we believed to be hidden there. We collected secret passages at that time as other children collected stamps or cigarette cards. Not that we ever found a real one, but even the most imaginary tunnel was as potent against intrusive adults as its real prototype would have been against Cromwell.

We could not speak of the passage in front of

Mummy so we simulated other interests. My brother threw stones; rebuked, he threw sticks. One came alive in his hand. It was a grass snake.

My mother behaved wonderfully. It was an unfortunate episode, rather bad form of the serpent, best to forget about it. She gave us each a sixpence with which to hire a toboggan at a nearby cottage. I adored tobogganing: I ran, I shrieked, I slid. But a voice inside me said: 'So we met at last!' It was the snake. I ran after tea to fetch Mummy's bag from her bedroom – 'Turn on the light, darling, you know where it is!' I could hear him behind me on the staircase, he slithered down the dark passage, and when, oh merciful electricity! a small click brought light and deliverance and the security of my mother's bedroom, his voice said, 'Wait till tonight!'

That night he was in my bed, his nakedness slithering under the bedclothes, his cold body tightening round mine. I knew if I called out he would kill me, so I never called out.

'You see, Nurse,' said my mother, 'she has learnt self-control.'

Every October brought Salisbury fair. Each year we begged to go to it, each year my mother prevaricated. Fairs meant gypsies and germs and skin-troubles. Gentry children were better away from them, especially when they took place in town market places and not on some nice clean village green. The year of the snake she relented. A young woman with too much life for her way of life, she was bored with Salisbury, and felt the roundabouts and flares and October sun in her impatient blood. Perhaps like the year she grew old reluctantly.

'Put on your best coats,' she cried on Nannie's day

out. 'We're certain to meet your cousins.'

It was not, we knew, at the fair, that we should meet them but on the way to the Cathedral. My mother, fearing an unexpected visit, had had the foresight to telephone and had been told by a shocked maid that it was a Saint's Day, so they would have a late tea and had had an early lunch.

Piety, my mother said, must be very trying to the digestion. She could not imagine how they got their maids to stay. Prunes on feast days and rice on fast days and never a meal at the right time. Which Saint's Day is it, Ronald wondered.

Skipping beside my mother in my best scarlet coat I thought perhaps it was mine. Perhaps I was a saint. Truly I felt happy enough to be one. It was my day of days. I rode to Heaven on the roundabouts, to Hell in the switchbacks. No longer a stolid child with one eye on eternity, I was for the first time part of life.

Paying my third penny to the gypsy in the engine I rode my golden horse and damned my foes. If only I had a shilling I might never have to climb down, the gypsy would think me a fixture. My dreams were broken by my brother whispering from an adjacent antelope that he felt sick. We withdrew terrified and sought the safer 'Hoopla'. Even here my luck held, my first ring circled a pink vase, my second a bottle of Californian Poppy. I could afford to be generous about my brother's coconuts, it was my day of days. I clasped my hideous vase passionately. I had won it, I could do something. I had ridden the golden horse, I had steered the scarlet motor car, I had found Heaven and a place of my own in Heaven.

My brother was fixated upon the coconuts, to him they meant more than pink vases, perhaps because they seemed more sporting. My mother stood beside him exclaiming dotingly and handing out large portions of the housekeeping money in threepences. I escaped to wander alone and illicitly in my new-found heaven. Suddenly I stopped short at a notice: 'To the Snake Pit 1*d*.'

I had a penny, I went to the snake pit. I had ridden a golden horse. I had won a vase. I was no longer alone and a failure. Too long I had been tyrannised by my enemy, now I would seek him out and look in his eyes and conquer him forever. Or so I dreamed. A woman caught my shoulder:

'Why 'tis Miss Helen, are you all right, dear? You almost toppled over. Does your Mummy know you're here?'

It was Mrs Dean who did sewing for us. I scarcely saw her for my eyes looked beyond her. In hideous tangle in a pit four foot by six lived all the horror in the world. Serpents were curled like wool in knitting – cobra – python – cobra, plain – purl. I had meant to confront my particular serpent but I could not see him. In abominable confusion alien head claimed alien tail. No serpent was separate, none owned his own part, all were part of filthiness. Unlike God's Holy One I had seen corruption. I fell at Mrs Dean's feet in what novelists then called 'a little crumpled heap'.

Childhood like Hades is tongueless. I had been to heaven on my golden horse, I had seen hell in the snake pit, but I had no words to tell. My mother was kind when the dressmaker found her. It was tiresome of me to have run away, the height was upsetting of course and then there had been all that roundabout riding. Ronald had won three more coconuts, it was time to go home.

We had tea for a treat by the fire in the drawing-room – macaroons for my brother, eclairs for me and hot buttered toast for everyone in honour of the first frost of the year.

I ate greedily but in my mind the serpents still knitted their purl-plain-purl. If only I had had words and could have told my mother, there in the firelight in the sane prettiness of that 1917 drawing-room, how easy would have been my future world! But I could not tell her and so the snake pit found a place in my mind with the things I could never tell.

Chief among these was tea with Mr O'Connell. Son of a family of some distinction, this eccentric lived in a Regency cottage a mile away, and loved children, especially little girls. I went to tea with him on alternate Wednesdays, pleased to find someone who preferred me to my brother. My host was a tall man about sixty with a drooping red moustache. His brother, who was mad and had to have his bread buttered by his keeper, had a red beard. Ronald, on the only occasion he had been invited, had been frightened by this, but I rather liked it. I liked beards and old men and gruff questions because I associated them with God and thought that if old men approved of me God would approve, and this was important as I felt I should surely die soon. Nannie had been reading *The Keeper of the Door* by Ethel M. Dell and the chapters I had absorbed when she was absent from the nursery made me think a great deal about death.

To return to Mr O'Connell, at the back of his study he kept a model of Salisbury Cathedral. It lived in a glass case and if I was good I was allowed to dust it with a paint brush. Much as I relished the omnipotent feeling of chasing bits of dust down the tiny aisles I should have relished it more but for the unpleasantness 'being good' entailed. To pay for the pleasures of ecclesiastical spring cleaning I was compelled to allow Mr O'Connell to press his wet red moustache in my mouth.

'It's queer how fond the old gentleman is of you!' Nannie would say as she fetched me. 'I hope you behaved like a lady.' And I would say, 'Yes, Nannie darling,' and hold her hand extra tightly, thinking with joy of the disinfectant with which I should rinse my mouth. I trusted her as much as I loved her and if I never told her of the moustache or the snakes it was because I feared to ruin forever the cheerful innocence of her world.

Since I have grown up I have known other adults with Nannie's innocence – with bread and jam minds and no nonsense – and because of Nannie I have always been fond of them. What I have never grown to care for is cathedrals. I do not ever remember feeling happy or at home in them except on that superb occasion when Salisbury Close flooded and Ronald and I punted up the Cathedral aisle on hassocks while my Mother said 'How terrible' to the Dean. I do not think she really thought it terrible, for the week before the flood he had commented unfavourably on the prints on our staircase.

'When you have been married as long as I have you will no doubt have some presentable pictures.'

I think that she thought that a just providence overhearing this quip had let the Avon into the Dean's territory; in any case she made no effort to control our boating and we had fine aquatic sport, watched jealously by the late Bishop's better trained children. I do not think I shall ever see anything so blissfully anarchic as that water. It swirled round the pillars, lolled up the aisle, drunkenly tilted the High Altar. Inspired by its irreverence, I ventured something I had never ventured before; steering my hassock carefully I escaped behind the Altar. Here would most certainly dwell the Holy of Holies, the Tabernacle of the Lord. I do not know why but I had persuaded myself that no one except the priest ever penetrated behind the High Altar. I thought that God lived there, probably in some sort of box, and that the priest came on Sundays and took Him out and then put Him back again. Written down like this it sounds a little crude and impious but ultimately it is not much odder than the real tenets of the Christian faith.

Unlike most believers I sought to put belief to the test. Deftly I punted between the pillars, round the pulpit, behind the Altar. If God were there and angry I should be sorry, but then we would have to meet sometime. God was not there. Instead there were effigies of lords and bishops, soggy hymnals and hassocks, and an emptiness I hope never to find again on earth.

I returned to my mother. Ronald had fallen in trying to ride two hassocks at once and was both wet and furious. We went out through the Great Door meeting the late Bishop's children returning with pails and brooms and scowls of indignation. I smiled at them benignly, smug in my new agnosticism. Poor innocents, how young they were! From that day forth I should be old.

When I was eighteen I went to fetch a friend at a Quaker meeting-house. It was a long white room with nothing remarkable in it and the worshippers stood in silence creating their church in their minds. When we came into the street my friend said, 'I expect you found it odd and empty with no choir or priest or altar.' Remembering that space behind Salisbury High Altar I told her I had seldom found a room so full.

'Poor children, dose no one care for them?' my mother asked rhetorically all the way home. She meant the late Bishop's children. Later when I grew up and married the youngest of them I realised that there had been nothing pitiful about them except that there had been a disproportionate number of children to nurse-maids and therefore their socks fell down. Their souls, unlike ours, were tended and no doubt these flowered.

My mother put her clothes on like a goddess and had a fine contempt for dowdy women. She liked to mimic the Bishop's wife, pulling the front of her skirt up, sticking out her stomach, and pushing an imaginary full pram. Probably the mimicry was the more zestful because the Bishop's wife was both beautiful and county, and on the only occasion that my mother had been invited to dinner at the Palace had forgotten all about it and gone to London, leaving my mother and father to expend their fury on a long-suffering butler and return home to a servantless house to cook scrambled eggs in tails and gold lamé with a train. Local gossip said that one morning the same butler slipped out of the Close for a port and came back to tell the Bishop's wife that he and the staff must give notice, they could no longer face the Palace food.

'But Craddock,' said the Bishop's wife, 'You eat the same food as his Lordship and I eat.'

'That,' said the poor butler, 'is precisely what the staff and I complain of.'

Once at the end of an inordinately long and frugal dinner a visiting bishop leant over to his secretary: 'Be so good as to fetch the packet of sandwiches in my suitcase in the hall.'

Apart from those slighted like my mother, Salisbury adored its genius Bishop, and even the Southern Railway officials relaxed their habitual grimness to wink at one another when, scorning to show his ticket, his Lordship reached the London train by vaulting through the Left Luggage hall. I wish he had not died before I was prelate-conscious, it would have been exciting to know a genius. His no less remarkable if less saintly widow lived till 1938 and became, as I have said, my mother-in-law. It is with an effort that I remain in 1917 and am not lured twenty-one years on by her beautiful and aristocratic voice demanding over the telephone of the fishmonger on Good Thursday if he thought Our Lord's Crucifixion an occasion for profiteering in cod. She was a matriarch of unusual power and ferocity, but it was my children's lives and not mine which were to be influenced by her.

It is very difficult to learn to live. It takes a long time to walk and talk and then there is that mysterious thing called poise. Childhood would be much less tortuous if grown-ups would extend to children the courtesy which Queen Victoria extended to the man who knifed his peas. If, by some fatal error, a common person had come to our house, our parents would not have called attention to his manner of eating... they never hesitated to call attention to ours.

'Take your elbows off the table. Stop fingering that bread. A napkin is not a handkerchief. Why speak with your mouth full?'

And finally, when the cannonade was over, 'It would be pleasant if the children could stir themselves to make polite conversation.'

It would indeed have been pleasant and we longed to please them but our best stories died on our lips. Dining-room food lost all its savour before it reached your mouth. We longed to go back to the nursery and make our mashed potato into ploughed fields. Nannie, it is true, worked hard with our table manners, but she managed to do it without making us feel we were sub-human and ought to eat on the floor.

More devastating even than table manners was the problem of deportment, more devastating that is, for me. My mother had decided that I hunched one shoulder. She confided her suspicion to my father with the result that I never entered a room without one or other of them shouting: 'Stand up straight – hold yourself properly – are you deformed?'

Soon I became convincd that I was. It became torture to meet strangers. The more I liked them the more I feared they should guess. My father's mother had died of a tubercular spine and I see now that his anxiety about my back was natural. He did not mean to be unkind. I think my mother did. She was a pretty vivacious woman married to a proud cold man and doomed to a life that was too quiet for her. Perhaps she dreaded to see her charms fade and was glad not to see them bloom in her daughter. I think she was relieved I was plain. Once when a charming visitor told her she thought I might grow up beautiful (plain child, lovely woman, was perhaps how she saw it) my mother was very angry and said:

'I see no signs of it but I am told she is clever, though I am sure I do not know what good that will be to her.'

I ran upstairs and told Nannie what the visitor had said.

'Do you think she could possibly be right, Nannie?

Will I be pretty?'

'Well, my lamb, I don't know why not – you've got pretty arms for evening dress and a nice back' – scrubbing me with a loofah.

'Mummy said it was nonsense.'

'Your Mummy,' Nannie said tartly, 'hasn't a monopoly of good looks.'

'What's monopoly?'

'Nothing. Forget it. Turn over and I'll wash your tummy.'

'Nannie, don't you like Mummy?'

'Of course I do. Now we don't want any more silly talk. Get out and I'll dry you.'

About this time my brother had toothache and it was arranged that to spare him the horrors of a dentist chair – he was only seven – the dentist should come to the house and take out the tooth in the comparative comfort of the spare room. All this was contrived in advance, and for days Ronald walked about untouchable and aloof. The least rebuke from Nannie or cross word from me reduced him to tears and Mummy arrived in the nursery to ask was she the only one with a heart in the house?

Actually Ronald was a manly boy but he wanted to please Mummy and for her the accent was seldom on Sparta.

At last the fateful day dawned. Ronald was not allowed any breakfast, which made the nursery meal rather indecent. He played bravely on the window sill until my mother swept in, dissolved into tears at the sight of his breakfastlessness, and took him downstairs ostensibly to see Cook but really to give him a clandestine banana.

The 'operation' was timed for eleven. Morbidly I

crept along the passage to the spare room which was unduly tidy and smelt strongly of Lysol, having been scrubbed with it from top to bottom. Mummy read Mrs Molesworth's *Carrots* aloud in the drawing-room.

Feeling superfluous and unheroic I went to the garden to find Reeves. At eleven Nannie found me and suggested that we should pick Ronald some strawberries. He might fancy them when it was over.

'Have they come yet?' I asked. 'They' were the doctor and dentist.

'Bless you,' said Nannie, 'it'll be over now.'

She was right. Winifred came running down the garden.

'He's come round. You can come.'

We tore into the house and up to the spare room.

At the door my heart sank. I do not know what horror I expected to see. Summoning up my courage I advanced across the threshold with my strawberries, Nannie followed with a jug of cream. Ronald lay on the large brass bed, looking much as he always looked. Doctor and dentist faced each other across him.

'I'm afraid there's no doubt about it, Poxford,' said the doctor, 'you have drawn the wrong tooth.'

'But you said the right,' said the dentist truculently.

'I meant his not yours.'

'Do you mean,' said my mother interrupting, 'that through your gross carelessness my precious must go through it all again. . .?'

'Certainly,' said Mr Poxford. 'And this time in the right place. Perhaps you will ring my secretary for an appointment. Can I give you a lift, Davenport?'

'What a very rude man,' said my Mother to the Doctor who had stayed behind to propitiate her. He had to stay because he was one of the four who played bridge at our house every Tuesday. She looked white and shaken. Suddenly she regained her usual poise and composure.

'Of course – I know why he spoke like that. I haven't called on Mrs Poxford. One must draw the line somewhere. Dental surgeon indeed – dentist he is and dentist he always will be!'

– 4 –

Snobbery was also responsible for my education or lack of it. Salisbury was fortunate enough to possess a gigantic and efficient girls' school to which was attached an excellent kindergarten run by a German lady called Miss Falwzzar. If gossip could intern or imprison, this saintly lady would have been behind bars, but so innocent was her demeanour that the local spy-maniacs who denounced her at dinner awoke in the morning thankful to consign their children to her care.

Miss Falwzzar may or may not have been pro-German, she was certainly pro-Heaven and I was fortunate to spend the first three years of my school life with a saint. I went to her kindergarten when I was six, my brother a year later. At home my mother alternately spoilt or scolded, at school we tied bows, sang hymns and collected wild flowers, under the eye of a detached and disinterested human being.

Miss Falwzzar had grey hair which scorned its bun, huge hands and a gaunt body. Her clothes were the least presentable I had ever seen. At lunch time when she stooped to tie my shoe laces my mother would sweep her with the fine darts of female patronage.

I have never yearned for any skill so much as I yearned to be able to tie those shoe laces, but the harder I tried the sillier did my fingers become. I longed to tie them both because I hated to see Miss Falwzzar kneel in the dust while my mother told her about her social successes and because I disliked my mother's assumption that because I could not do things with my fingers I was deficient in my brain.

'I hope you find her "all there"?' my mother asked the first day.

Miss Falwzzar frowned at the idiom.

'My husband and I often wonder whether she is normal,' my mother explained. 'She can do nothing for herself at all. Look at her now. Six years old and can't tie a bow!'

'When Miss Douglas came on her annual visit to us this morning,' said Miss Falwzzar, 'Helen was able to spell orange. I hope she will be an earnest pupil, I am sure she is a clever one.'

Miss Douglas was the head of the big school. Every day we trooped into its great hall for Intercession for the Forces at eleven o'clock. She was small and shabby, and holy beyond words. What is more she was of good family and though my mother knew nothing of what six hundred girls felt when she said, 'Lift up your heads O ye gates,' and we answered, 'And lift ye up your everlasting doors,' she knew she was a Rutlandshire Douglas and could not be patronised like a poor German. She was not particularly impressed by Miss Falwzzar's opinion of me, but she questioned me in the pony trap about Miss Douglas.

'Did she ask you how I was? Didn't she know who you were? How did she treat Doreeen Rogers?'

This last was the chemist's daughter who in spite of keen local opposition shared our studies.

I explained that Miss Douglas had swept in, looked

at our raffia work, inspected the Plasticene model of Jerusalem, said a prayer about God's grace, and on the way out asked suddenly if anyone could spell orange. Oddly enough I could, and she had said, 'What is your name, child?' and when I had told her had bade me 'Learn to love God and knowledge.'

My mother observed she was a funny old thing, perhaps 'past it'. There was talk of having someone younger, who would think more of games and the social side. Miss Douglas, although a lady, had let it get beyond her – chemist's daughters and all that. Besides there was the question of the Fox-Trot. Better to have someone younger and more up-to-date.

The Fox-Trot question was indeed a vexed one. Throughout the war years every Tuesday the gentry children of Salisbury assembled at three o'clock in the school hall to be taught dancing by a lady from London. In theory anyone who could pay the fees was admitted, in practice it was made very uncomfortable for any tradespeople's children who might attend. Having gatecrashed the kindergarten the chemist's family thought the dancing class child's play. They were wrong. Saints know nothing of class distinction, and Miss Falwzzar found English life puzzling anyway, but Miss Peters who taught dancing knew all about class. A visitor from another county could have guessed from the voice she used to bid this or that child do her clubs alone how many hundreds of Wiltshire acres its father owned.

Unhappily for Miss Peters, the chemist's daughter was an excellent dancer. Throughout the long afternoon from skipping to clubs, through the twenty positions of the hands to step-dancing, and finally through the intricacies of the waltz and one-step,

Doreen shone, making her social superiors look like cart-horses. Even so Miss Peters would find a way never to praise Doreen, and when at last we would line up to make our final curtseys she would contrive to make her feel that as she could never hope to make the sole curtsey in the world that mattered her grace was superfluous.

'A little top-heavy, Belinda, not quite so dainty as your sister's last week. Ah yes, I saw her in the *Tatler*, Lady Blakeney, a sweet dress! . . . Gently, gently, Petronelle, remember this is the ballroom not the stables! Though I must say' (this to Petronelle's tweedy mother) 'many a good marriage is made in a loose box . . . . Well, Doreen, what are you waiting for? There are three young ladies behind you. Am I not to have the honour of your curtsey?'

To go back to the Fox-Trot. This new dance was at the height of its first favour. Miss Peters longed to teach it to us. Miss Harvey, her young and fashionable (if scarcely lady-like) assistant had already won one competition, but Miss Douglas was adamant. No Godolphin School child should Fox-Trot. Waltzes were one thing, one-steps perhaps socially necessary, but to Fox-Trot meant perdition. It should not be taught in the school hall.

My mother who hated to be beaten had a clever idea. She and my father were enthusiastic dancers, the floor in our drawing-room excellent, she offered hospitality for the night to Miss Peters and Miss Harvey in return for tuition in the Fox-Trot for herself and my father. As the craze proceeded my brother and I came to be fetched down in our dressing gowns for secret instruction. Soon we were Miss Peters' favourites. Hearing her speak to us at the dancing class a stranger would have guessed we had a grouse moor. The Fox-Trot question was answered, at least for us; there remained the chemist's daughter. The more my mother saw her the less she liked her. For one thing she danced so much better than I did, for another the susceptible Ronald had fallen for her.

Ronald, of course, danced exquisitely. At five his technique was so good that Miss Peters asked if he might dance for charity at a Savoy matinée. My father was appalled by the unmanliness of the idea, but he need not have worried. Ronald danced like a boy not a girl. Soon he was the beau of the class, rivalled only by two small Scots who wore kilts, did the sword dance and possessed a ducal uncle. I delighted and surprised my mother by charming the elder Scot who read poetry and kept a deerhound, but even this could not efface the disgrace of Ronald and Doreen. My mother could not endure it. She had headaches on Tuesdays and sent Nannie to chaperone us. Once Nannie was ill and we went with Bertha, the nursemaid. When the class was over it was discovered that our cab had not come. It was raining dismally, my brother shivered and sneezed at the door. Seeing our predicament, the chemist's wife bore down upon us kindly. We could share her cab to the market place and when we reached the shop either telephone about ours or take theirs on.

Bertha was too callow to be class-conscious, besides she was frightened by Ronald's sneeze. We were bustled into the cab by the triumphant Mrs Peters, and before we had noticed the enormity of what we had done, were examining the coloured liquid in the bottles behind the counter and helping fat Mr Peters sell Cachet Faivre and Allenbury's Infant Foods.

It all took a long time though Bertha had the sense to

refuse tea, and we were getting out of the cab when my father arrived back from the office. Even if we had had the tact not to tell him our bulging pockets would have spoken for us, for Mr Peters had laden us with Blackcurrant Pastilles and Allenburys Milk Chocolate; having no tact we rushed to inform him:

'Daddy, you'll never guess! I sold Mrs Murray some senna pods, and Major Graham a bottle of aspirin. I wish *you* had a chemist's shop!'

The next morning when we went down to the dining-room to say goodbye to Daddy and to eat the superb bonne bouche of toast and butter and marmalade he always saved for us, he told us gravely that he and our mother would spend the week-end inspecting schools. The present arrangements were no longer suitable.

It was a pity because this term, the Fox-Trot one, I had raised myself from the kindergarten to the bottom form of the big school. I had spent an acutely unhappy few weeks losing myself in long disinfectant-smelling corridors and being snubbed by everyone for asking reasonable questions but it had been a purposeful misery. Or so I had thought. Miss Falwzzar had spoilt me at the kindergarten, letting me be the May Queen and Britannia in pageants and insisting, to the fury of the Bishop's wife, that I chose the hymns. As I only knew *Eternal Father* and *Onward Christian Soldiers* the fury of the Bishop's wife was justified. Her son would have chosen so much better. But, in spite of the spoiling, Miss Falwzzar had taught me to work and as the youngest of six hundred girls I enjoyed my new-found adulthood. I did not want to be a child any more. I wore my hideous gym tunic with determined pride and was delighted when my mother castigated it. I did not want to wear pretty clothes or be a lady but to know all knowledge and be like Miss Douglas, if a mortal could be like a goddess.

Perhaps my mother guessed my ambition and thought it kinder to thwart it at nine than at nineteen. I could not be a bluestocking if I was not taught. Devoutly she scoured the country for establishments where learning had less place in the curriculum than deportment, good health and home comforts. She was brilliantly successful. Fieldend, the school she ultimately selected, had no trained person on its staff except the games mistress, and its headmistress boasted that none of her girls were encouraged to think themselves clever. My mother liked it because the uniform was pretty (not common like black stockings and gym tunics), the girls had good manners, and it had the supreme advantage of being opposite the excellent preparatory school my father had chosen for my brother. It would be nice for us to be able to wave to each other and we would share the same chapel.

But before we left for boarding school there was the Armistice. On 10 November 1918 Ronald had his middle finger shut in the door by the gardener's boy. The top of it fell off and floated like a toy boat in the washing-up bowl full of blood. I wept, Cook screamed, Nannie nearly fainted, and it was left to the admirable Reeves to hold the bowl while Mummy telephoned the doctor. When, at last he came, it was only to torture Ronald more. He came back every three hours for dressings and I grew to hate him. Ronald seemed very small and white and heroic and the household was so spent with his pain that when the next morning after breakfast Daddy put down the telephone and said 'The war is over' no one had the strength to care. However at the beginning of lessons it was customary to sing a verse of a hymn and I leapt to my feet to ask the form mistress whether we should choose one about victory.

'Certainly not, it would be premature.'

'But the Armistice has been signed this morning.'

'Nonsense. It is very wicked to tell lies.'

'But, Miss Cook, my father says it has.'

'Your father is a very distinguished citizen, Helen Fletcher, but he is not the Prime Minister.'

Miss Douglas told the school the news when we met for intercession at eleven. I waited hopefully for my form mistress to apologise. She never did and it cured me of ever wanting to know news first. To this day I do not know where my father got his information.

Our household had its private woe. Ronald, very white and heroic, seemed to have no time to recover after the cruel dressings before the now hated doctor arrived again. Had there been strawberries and cream in England in this wartime November he should have had them, but this time his plight was beyond the beguilements of strawberries and cream. The doctor, an old family one accustomed to our adulation, and loathing his new role of torturer, besought my mother to take Ronald away before he suffered mental as well as physical hurt:

'Take him to London, my dear lady. They're riding on the top of taxis I hear, and blowing trumpets. Take him to London and let him blow one and drink champagne too if he likes it. It'll take the little chap's mind off his finger.'

So Ronald went with Mummy to London and I who had no bad finger stayed in Salisbury. I expect that in spite of the justice I thought the arrangement cruel but I can remember nothing about the Armistice celebrations in Salisbury though I am sure they were prodigious. My mind was occupied exclusively with thoughts of the new school and how to be the most popular girl in it. I ate and slept in a world of Angela Brazil.

In retrospect it is surprising that November 1918 should have found a normally intelligent ten-year-old girl with her mind centred entirely on her school uniform. I suppose like war-wearied England I wanted to be reborn. I had not been a success in tussore smocks or in kilts and jerseys; perhaps I should be another person in the brown tweed dress with the white collar (and cuffs for church and lectures) which were the uniform of the new school.

Although my mother and Cook and the colonels who had stayed with us had thought us tragic figures, my brother and I had been actually very little affected by the war. When an English plane nose-dived in flames in a field near the house we had stood with the maids while the young man was burnt to death in it, and waited by the ashes till the fire engine arrived from Salisbury belatedly, and with it my mother to recall the maids to their duties and Nannie to her normal sanity. I was tormented by the thought that the young man had cried out and we had done nothing, but the maids seemed more than satisfied with their part in the affair, and by the evening were regarding themselves as heroines.

For the rest I remember my mother leaning on Daddy's arm and weeping by the herbaceous border and telling us something had happened to Kitchener. Someone had buried a beloved horse on one side of the border and I often sat on its grave and thought tragically about it. I found the sorrows and deaths of animals more moving than the disasters of human beings.

Sometimes children from London came to stay because of the air-raids. David Burnaby's son John came once without his nurse and I remember we admired the adult way in which he asked Nannie to manicure his nails. We had to run across the gravel to fetch our outdoor shoes which Charlie cleaned in the harness room, but John would stand on the back step and call out imperiously, 'Bring my shoes here, boy! My feet will get wet!'

We admired his commanding manner and envied his theatrical background. I tried leaning back in the armchair in the hall and drawling, 'Lace up my boots, at once, Nannie!' but the experiment was spoilt by her demanding, 'Who will lace them for you when you grow up?'

'Why, I shall be rich and have ladies' maids.' I dwelt importantly on the plural.

'Someone will have to marry you first and I don't suppose they will if you're not pretty,' said Ronald, annilihating all my dreams. He meant to be helpful not unkind. I was not pretty and my failure to be efficient or domesticated was the talk of the household. Everyone marvelled that such a homemaker as my mother could have had such a daughter. When we went down to the kitchen to help make our own milk puddings – my brother liked his milky and I preferred mine toffee, and it was thought that helping to cook them might make us eat them up better – it was he and not I who showed culinary prowess. If we went into the pantry to help my mother arrange flowers Ronald's were works of art while mine were stuck in too deep or I put pink flowers next to red, a crime which my mother regarded as unpardonable.

On Thursdays when we inspected the maids' bedrooms, a task that afforded my mother much righteous pleasure – 'Windows shut again. . . Hairpins on the floor. . . . Surely that's my chemise. . . . Really, can Winifred never use a hair-tidy?' – I always felt an interloper and ashamed. I disliked the way my mother dabbed extra 4711 on her handkerchief on the way upstairs, and detested her smug assumption that anyone who was not a lady smelt.

I had begun by this time to discredit her oral as well as her social judgments, and this brings me to my only profound realisation of the pain of war.

Among the various officers billeted on us (there were never less than two, and these were generally important as the house was more than usually comfortable and very near the camps) was Major Drake. He was six foot four and into each of his inches was injected liking to live. All the billeted officers gave us presents but when Major Drake gave me even a chocolate I was assured I was a princess. All the grown-ups in the house loved him as much as we did and when he came up to the nursery Nannie relaxed all the rules.

One day Major Drake asked if he might take us into the New Forest to see his sister. My mother teased him, saying what would he do all day with two small children, but in reality we were big, or anyhow big enough to go to the lavatory alone which is all that grown-ups mean in that context. Clearly my mother would have preferred to be asked as well but it was a very small car and Major Drake kept saying his sister's house was small.

It was a very hot morning and we were washed and sleeked and dressed in our new tussore coats from

Gorringes. Nannie's efforts were in vain because in three miles Ronald had chocolate all over his face and I had acid drops in my pigtails. When we reached Ringwood Major Drake stopped feasting us and changed his teasing voice to a grave one.

'Can you two keep a secret?'

We answered, remembering the Royalist passage, that we had kept hundreds.

'Well,' said Major Drake, 'Pamela, the lady we are going to see, is not my wife.'

'But you said,' said Ronald, 'she was your sister.'

'That,' said Major Drake, 'is the secret. She is not my wife or my sister. She is the lady I love. You must promise not to tell your mother.'

We promised and the green glades of the Forest became pregnant with mystery and adventure. Soon we came to a small white cottage with heart-shaped windows. It looked like the sugar cottage in *Hansel and Gretel*. Pamela, however, did not look like a witch. Looking back I suppose she was beautiful; at that time and with only the chocolate-box charmers of Salisbury to compare her with, I could find no words to describe her. All the women who came to our house wanted to please men. Pamela looked as though she wanted men to please her and as though Major Drake did please her.

'Why, Paul,' she said in a very low voice when he kissed her, 'you haven't introduced me to your friends.'

Major Drake introduced us fully and with dignity. No one had ever done that before. People had said, 'So these are the children,' or 'A girl and a boy, how nice!' but no one had introduced us. We were impressed.

'I expect Helen would like to come up to my bedroom,' Pamela said when we reached the front door. 'You take Ronald with you.'

On the way upstairs she showed me the lavatory and gave me a pink visitor's towel to dry my hands on. In the bathroom the soap smelt of carnations.

'Come here and I'll comb that lovely smooth hair,' she called as I hesitated in the doorway.

I went across the pink carpet and stood by the dressing table, fascinated by the array of silver brushes and scent bottles.

'Mummy,' I said dubiously, 'always wishes I had curls.'

She laughed and turned my face to the light.

'No, Helen, curls would spoil you. If you were my daughter I would want you smooth not curly.'

'I wish,' I said devoutly, 'that I were your daughter. I should like to stay here always.'

'That is a very nice thing to say. Now we must have our lunch. Do you think your brother will like lobster? I had not realised he would be so small.'

On the table there was melon in tall glasses. Major Drake had picked a white rose.

'Ronald and I picked this because we thought it looked like you.'

It was true, Pamela did look like a rose. She did not seem surprised at being told so but said, 'Thank you, Paul and Ronald. Now Paul, pour out the wine. Shall we give Helen and Ronald some in their water, and pretend we are having lunch in France?'

Ronald did not like his lobster so Pamela fetched him cold chicken from the kitchen. There were no maids and she seemed to like waiting on us. I thought she was more like a princess pretending to be parlour maid than a grown-up woman being domesticated. There were strawberries in a silver bowl and more cream than we had ever seen at once.

'But Pamela,' said Major Drake, 'where did you find it? You must be a witch.'

'Oh, a nice farmer gave it to me. Everyone is so kind.'

'Do you mean you didn't have to pay for it?' Ronald asked practically. 'Mummy says it costs a lot to get cream in war time.'

'Oh Pamela never pays for anything,' said Major Drake, 'she is so beautiful she has only to smile.'

'Do you think what he said was true?' Ronald asked, as we rested on a huge mahogany bed with muslin curtains.

'Well, it's certainly true that she's beautiful.'

'Not more beautiful than Mummy and she has to pay for cream!'

'Don't you two want to get up?' Major Drake asked, putting his head round the door. 'Helen, you're a lady, or soon going to be, go and see why Pamela is so long powdering her nose. I want to walk in the Forest.'

I ran to Pamela's room, intrigued that after all my mother's talk about how wicked it was, I should at last see someone powdering their nose.

Pamela was not powdering her nose now but instead she was sitting at her dressing-table crying. Every now and then she would take a very small handkerchief and dab her face dry, but always in a few seconds it was wet again.

'Please try my handkerchief,' I begged. 'It was clean when Nannie gave it me this morning.'

'Pamela took it and blew her nose, avoiding politely the acid drop sticky. Suddenly she did not seem like a grown-up. She put her head on my shoulder.

'Oh Helen, did you know he is going to France

tomorrow? I love him so much, too much. Oh child, why do they make wars?'

She looked at her face in the glass. 'We can't let him see me like this. Quick, what shall I do? I know, you run into the bathroom and put this handkerchief under the cold tap. If they say anything say my nose is bleeding.'

I did as she said and we spread it over her face. Then she did things with powder and cream and put on some sharp scent that was neither lavender water nor 4711.

'I thought ladies didn't use powder or scent,' I asked, to take her mind off the crying.

She laughed. 'Is that what they teach you in Salisbury, you funny infant? Still perhaps you are right, perhaps I am not a lady, or anyhow not the Salisbury sort of lady.'

'Then in that case I shan't try to be one,' I said stoutly. 'I want to grow up just like you, though of course I won't ever be beautiful like you.'

'Silly child, you'll be lovely, and you'll grow up in a good world where there won't be any wars.'

When she said war I was frightened she might cry again so I took her downstairs and we found Ronald and Major Drake and went into the Forest. There were deer and shaggy ponies and foals that looked wet and sticky. Major Drake tried to catch one for Pamela to hold but it staggered to its impossible-looking legs and ran off. We went back to the cottage for tea. It was China and we drank it out of elegant cups with flowers on them because no one had ever told Pamela that children drink milk in mugs.

After tea we went into the garden to play while Pamela and Major Drake talked in the house. Gradually the shadows grew longer and blacker, soon

Ronald fell asleep in the hammock. I was frightened because I knew we should be at home in bed and there were no lights in the house and I could not hear voices. I felt as if I had fallen out of a dream. I climbed into the hammock beside Ronald and I suppose I went to sleep too because when I woke up I was beside Major Drake in the front of the car and Ronald was asleep in the back seat wrapped in rugs.

'I wish I had said goodbye,' I said sleepily.

'Don't wish that, wish you'll never say it.'

I suppose I went to sleep again because when I woke we were at our own front door and Mummy was opening it and saying, instead of 'Have you had a nice time, darlings?' 'Really this is too much, Major Drake. My husband is waiting for you in the smoking room.'

'We had wine and strawberries and cream and Helen ate lobster,' Ronald told Nannie sleepily as she washed his face and hands. Ten o'clock was too late for baths.

'Lobster and wine, well I never! She'll have nightmares. Major Drake's sister should know better, but there, these unmarried ladies. . . .'

Nannie was disposed to feel tolerant now she had her darlings back.

'It wasn't Major Drake's sister. . . ,' Ronald began but I interrupted him.

'Oh Nannie, she was the loveliest lady! I won't have nightmares but perhaps I'll dream about her.'

'Well, Major Drake's a fine gentleman. You'd expect his sister to be handsome.'

'Major Drake is not a gentleman and the lady was not a lady nor was she his sister.' My mother had come into the nursery bathroom looking angrier than I had ever seen her. 'It is Mr Fletcher's wish, Nurse, that none of us ever mention Major Drake's name again. As for you, children, if you want to please me you will forget everything you have seen and heard today.'

I suppose I did not want to please her because I have never forgotten. I lay awake for a long time that night listening to my mother telling Nannie it was lucky we were so innocent. If we had been a few years older it might have had a terrible effect, especially on the girl. I do not remember Nannie saying much except, 'Fancy that, and such a sweet gentleman', and making her Tch Tch noise which I knew meant that she was not so cross as she thought she should be. I did not dream of the Forest lady but when I woke everything that had happened was stamped on my mind like a dream that has been dreamed many times.

For a day or two the grown-ups treated us as though we were in quarantine or had seen a dog run over, but gradually the special feeling wore off and I suppose they forgot. Ronald, who never did what Mummy asked him not to behind her back because of Honour, never spoke of our day in the Forest so I began to think it had happened only to me and was entirely mine. When my mother's friends said it was a pity my hair wouldn't curl I would smile in a secret way which made her very angry. I would pray for Major Drake's safety each night, murmuring his name in my prayers so that my mother would be curious and ask, 'What is that you say?' and I would have the incomparable pleasure of answering, 'I am forbidden to say it out loud.'

Someone told me about this time how the Jacobites drank secret toasts to the King over the Water and whenever anyone gave me a drink other than milk or water which both seemed unsuitable for toast drinking, I would say 'Pamela and Major Drake' and do odd things with my glass.

When on 11 November Miss Douglas announced the Armistice and everyone wept and sang *Land of Hope and Glory* I thought, 'Now he can go back to her!' and felt exalted as though I had won a private war, until one day at tea the Vicar's wife asked my mother, 'Did you ever hear any more of that tall young man I liked so much? the one who seemed so young to be a major. Wasn't his name Nelson?'

'Drake,' said my mother. 'Missing presumed dead.' She put on her tragedy voice. 'I had such a sweet letter from his wife in New Zealand, thanking me for all I had done for him. Poor thing, if only she knew. . . but thereby hangs a story. Helen, what are you gaping at? Go and fetch your sewing.'

– 5 –

My uncles, who had Lancashire coal mines, discovered in 1918 that they had failed to avoid making money out of the war. They, or rather their ancestors, had owned the mines since 1608 and truly wanted to deal justly with the miners. My grandfather had been the first English coalowner to install pit baths. His sons had therefore been shocked rather than pleased to find they had profited however inadvertently by 1914-18 and sought to find a good way of spending what they thought to be bad money. Later they gave Ronald and me £450 a year each, now they stood by to help with the problem of our education.

I say all this before dealing with Fieldend because the reader will say compassionately, 'Perhaps it was all her parents could afford.' They would be wrong. No money was spared. My father's family were just: of his five brothers and one sister only the suitable had been sent to Oxford and the sister, the much maligned Aunt Molly, had been one of the suitable. Similarly my father did not want to save on his daughter. He wanted to deal generously and justly with both of us. I suppose he had become so accustomed to his wife's silliness that he no longer noticed it and it never occurred to him to guess that there were schools designed to produce fresh female generations of the mental stature of my mother.

I am certain he did not want his only daughter to grow up like her, and if anyone had put it to him rationally he would have taken vigorous steps to prevent it.

It was not until I was seventeen and they parted that I realised how well, if shyly, he would have brought me up, but it was too late by then. I do not mean he would have wanted me to become what my mother called a bluestocking, but he would have wanted me to be free to choose a personality for myself. He combines conventionality and tolerance with a felicity that is, I suppose, the result of a classical education.

I had been an obscurely delicate little girl, catching everything and having it badly. Through recurrent crises of diphtheria, whooping cough, pneumonia, my body was dosed and massaged and coaxed back to health. We had a diet wise beyond the usual in those years, exercise, fresh air, fruit, Daniel Neal sandals; oculists, dentists, doctors, specialists were at hand when occasion arose. In all the affairs of the body my mother was knowledgeable beyond her period. My body has a great deal to thank her for, but my mind cries out against her in frustration and anger. If my mental development was intolerable to her could she not have let me develop away from her? It was cruel to let Miss Fleming continue at Fieldend the repression she had begun at home so well. But the hatred the Kitty Fletchers of this world feel for the intellect is implacable.

If I had a daughter she should not go to Fieldend, but Fieldend would still be there for her to go to. So much that is beautiful and good has perished in England since 1918 that it seems odd that a rather expensive home school with no qualified staff and no ideals to speak of, unless producing marriageable girls can be called an ideal, should still be thriving on its seaside hill. I do not know whether to marvel more that there are so many Miss Flemings to one Sappho or so many Kitty Fletchers to each well-balanced parent.

My brother and I were relieved when at last the day came to go to school. We had been at least twice to every treat Salisbury could provide, ranging from *Jack and Jill* at the Palace Theatre and *She Stoops to Conquer* at the New to *The Whip* at the already thriving Picture House. I remember the last especially because at the tensest moment when everything hangs on the race-horse racing the train Ronald always cried, and I never really learnt which won because for some odd reason I could not be left in the seats by myself while he was comforted in the tea lounge. Anyway all gaiety seemed a little tinny when faced with that yawning Harrods trunk. There was too that terrible business of goodbyes. My mother insisted that we should say one to everybody.

'You won't be seeing Miss Helen and Master Ronald any more,' she would say to the charwoman, or the assistant in the draper's or the waitress in the cake shop. 'They are going to boarding school.' And either they would look at us as if we were about to be executed – 'Poor little dears and so young!' – or as though we were unjustly privileged and ought to be guillotined – 'Well, I wish I'd had your chances! Nobody ever educated me!'

It was embarrassing either way, and we were glad when it was over. The last morning we woke to find Nannie crying as she pulled on her stays under her decorous flannel dressing-gown. She usually told us to shut our eyes or turn the other way, but now she was leaving and perhaps she didn't care any more. In the day nursery Ben, who never came upstairs, was nuzzling at the Harrods trunks. The sight of him standing there bewildered and unrebuked by Nannie or Bertha was the final proof that anarchy was loose upon the earth. In the garden I commended all the animals to a weeping Reeves. He had never sent any of his children away, and he had brought up twelve. I think he thought our parents depraved and cruel. Cook had already expressed her grief in sweets and cakes, Winifred was sorry she had ever chased me with slugs and snails, Bertha was weeping over the penny bazaar engagement ring Ronald had given her. My mother spent the after-breakfast period ringing everyone up:

'Yes, they are off today. . . . Yes, this afternoon. . . . Oh broken-hearted. . . . No they don't feel it much. . . . At least not so much as I do. . . . I cried all night. Stephen said I was foolish, men have no hearts of course. Well, I suppose it's for the best. Here is Helen. She can't leave my side, the poor child. Neither of them can. . . . She will speak to you herself. Tell Mrs Harrigan what you feel like, Helen!'

The rest of Fieldend and Derrington travelled direct from Waterloo. As we lived within motoring distance we were to go in a hired car with our mother and arrive before our school mates. We were glad because it saved a farewell scene with the station master and because it was exciting to drive so far. The doctor had not returned Daddy's car when the war stopped but Mummy said we should have one by next holidays. Actually the forty-mile drive in the landaulette was tedious and trying. We had eaten little of the farewell chicken and chocolate pudding at half past twelve and when we reached Swanage my mother suggested an early tea at the Grosvenor Hotel. Somehow this seemed impossible when we had been there so often on better occasions so we said firmly, 'Let's go now and get it over.'

We took my brother first. There was a drawing room like any Salisbury drawing-room among passages that smelt like corridors in hospitals. The headmaster's wife was cheerful on purpose, like the matron of Salisbury when I had gone there not to give tea but to have my arm X-rayed. It seemed worse than a hospital when Mummy wanted to see Ronald's bed and we went upstairs with Matron. There were seven iron bedsteads, each with a chair and a rug. No pictures except one of Jesus and a lamb over the empty fireplace.

'Of course it doesn't look like this when the boys are back,' Matron said. 'You should see the mess when they come off the train.'

She sounded as though she wished they would never come back or there would be a train smash.

'If there is anything you would like to tell me about Roland. Has he any habits?'

'Ronald, not Roland,' said my mother in her I-am-a-lady-but-don't-try-me-too-far voice.

'These fancy names!' said Matron. 'He'll be Fletcher here unless the boys don't like him and find some funny nicknames. Last term we had one called Big Ears and of course there are always Carrots and Fattys. You were saying about his habits?'

'How interesting your life must be. I always say it takes courage to look after other people's children.' She began to talk about the dreams and Sir William Bragg.

'O dreams . . . I meant does he wet his bed or. . . .' She drew my mother towards the lavatory door.

'Certainly not,' said my mother. 'I have never heard of such a thing and Nurse would most certainly have told me. I do not think you can be speaking of children from good homes.'

Left alone my brother and I gazed out of the window at Fieldend and across it at Swanage Bay. We felt suddenly very fond of each other.

I am glad I didn't bring my teddy,' he said.

'I daresay it won't be too awful,' I said hopefully. 'Anyway we can always run away. Look, we can signal each other from the windows.'

There was comfort in this.

'Come along, no whispering in corners!' Matron shouted. 'I always say,' she added more confidentially to my mother, 'take care of the tone and the health will take care of itself.'

My mother, who appeared to be not so sure about this, began to talk about Ronald's adenoids. At the bottom of the stairs a new boy with red hair was waiting with his mother. I could tell by the way my mother spoke when Mrs Grey introduced them that they were common, or as my mother's friends had all been drawling lately, 'Nouveau riche'. Ronald had begun to cry and it looked for one happy moment as if my mother had changed her mind about sending us to boarding school. Mrs Grey gave Ronald a look of scorn and said something about it always being better when goodbyes are over. Anyway it would be nice for Ronald to have his sister at Miss Fleming's. Lots of the boys had sisters there. . . a most delightful school.

'Come along now, no time for moping, kiss your mother and tell her we'll make a man of you by the time she sees you again.' This from Matron and all in one breath. I had just the time to see Ronald wince as she grabbed his shoulder before the door closed. My mother and I stood on the steps united in fury.

'Really,' said my mother, 'I cannot conceive why your father thought it a good school. . . . It's all the fault of your Uncle Frank.' (She meant Frank Fletcher of Charterhouse.) 'Though why he should think he knows better when he has no children! It's unnatural.' We climbed into the car and she wept a little. 'That matron. . . .' Soon the hired chauffeur was a party to our indignation. Unmarried women were the devil, now he had a sister. . . . My school was forgotten. Dusk fell as we planned to rescue Ronald.

'Don't you think,' I ventured at last, 'that I ought to go?'

'Why yes, of course. Give me my mirror. Do I look all right? I don't want the Miss Flemings to see I have been crying, spiteful old cats.'

'But I thought you said they were nice.'

'No schoolmistresses are nice or they'd be married. Let me comb your hair. You had better look like a lady's child even if no one expects you to behave like one.'

I guessed it was what Matron had said that rankled. 'What did Matron mean?' I asked.

'I don't know and I hope you'll never know.'

We rang the bell at Miss Fleming's. 'Mrs Fletcher and Miss Helen Fletcher,' said my mother firmly.

'Come in, Madam,' said the maid, 'Miss Fleming is expecting you.' She looked human and nice. My mother relaxed a little.

Miss Fleming and her sister, who seemed to be called Miss Amy, had clearly waited tea for us, or anyway for my mother.

'Perhaps Helen would like some too, as the other girls are not here yet.'

I was not accustomed to seeing grown-ups eat

without me and I said I would. Something in my voice made Miss Amy ask, 'Is she used to other children?'

'Well she has a brother,' my mother said, 'And she's been to school.'

'Oh, day school,' said Miss Amy in a voice that implied it did not count much.

'I am glad she is not an only child,' said Miss Fleming. 'They feel it more.'

My mother gave a little cry.

'Forgive me, a terrible thing has happened. I have just left my son across the road at Derrington and I have suddenly thought I have not given the poor darling any pocket money. Perhaps if you give me an envelope the chauffeur could run across the road with it.'

Miss Fleming provided an envelope and, more grudgingly, a piece of notepaper which my mother quickly covered with her fine bold handwriting, making grunts of satisfaction as she did so.

'I have told him he need not stay if they are unkind to him,' she told me triumphantly, putting two pound notes into the envelope and licking it viciously.

'Helen will not need as much as that,' said Miss Fleming, on whom the scene had had a most deleterious effect. 'She will scarcely need money except for stamps.'

My mother rose, adjusting her skunks.

'I expect I had better go. Well, be a brave girl, darling, and try to be happy.'

'Happiness isn't everything, that's what I always tell them,' said Miss Amy brightly.

'Perhaps you would like to see where she is going to sleep?' said Miss Fleming. 'And then you can hand her over to Matron.'

'No I must go.' My mother had had enough of Matrons for one day. She pressed a pound note into my hand, murmuring that I could always write for more. I tried to put it in my coat pocket and discovered that Harrods had sewn it up.

Miss Fleming held out her hand. 'I hope, Amy, we shall not find Helen deceitful.'

Miss Amy went to the bottom of the stairs and called, 'Matron!'

Miss Fleming put my pound note into a drawer in her desk, and gave me a shilling.

'I see', she said, 'you have always been a spoilt little girl. There are no spoilt girls here. Learn to take the rough with the smooth. Really, Matron, why are you not in uniform? The train will be in soon. Here is our new boarder.'

Matron was not at all like the arch-fiend at Derrington. Turning to look at her on the staircase, I saw a fat little woman in a black lace blouse and a great many bracelets. Directly we were out of hearing she began to grumble about the Miss Flemings and to tell me the hundred reasons why she had not put on her uniform. I knew she was not a lady and I liked her. I knew the Miss Flemings were ladies and I hated them both.

'Beautiful packing, beautiful!' she said as she took the tray out of the trunk.

'Yes,' I said loyally. 'Nannie did it.' Tears came into my eyes.

'Never mind,' said Matron. 'I will look after you. Mrs Green will be your friend. I could see your mother was a fine lady. I watched you come from my window. What a lovely coat she had on! It must have cost a lot of money. You tell your Mummy when you write that

Matron will look after you. She knows how a young lady should be treated.'

She pressed my hand in her hot wet hands. I did not like the feel of them but I was glad she liked me. Together we began to check my underclothes.

The dormitories were called after the Waverley novels. There were three white beds in Kenilworth, one of which Mrs Green said was mine. The other two, now untenanted, belonged to Priscilla le Mesurier and Ruth Jennings. Mrs Green said they had been here a year and were great friends. They were eleven. Although I was only ten they had not put me in Waverley, the junior dormitory, because my mother had said I was big for my age. Here Mrs Green paused and leered knowingly. If I grew much bigger she would have to put me in Peveril with the thirteen-year-olds who had cubicles.

Kenilworth had more human touches than Ronald's dormitory. There were pink mats and pink chintz curtains. Each girl had a small white chest of drawers with a mirror and a washstand attached to it. I could put my photographs on the dressing table part, Mrs Green said. I unpacked a huge enlargement of Ben with a tennis ball in his mouth and put it beside my hairbrush.

Mrs Green said that the housemaid would brush my hair every evening and my mother would pay extra. She, herself, would not have time to look after it. Long plaits looked very pretty but at boarding school they were a responsibility.

Suddenly there was an appalling commotion. The girls had arrived from the station. Remembering Angela Brazil, I felt like an actress on whom all the curtains in the world had gone up at once, but before I had had time to pose suitably Priscilla and Ruth had rushed in, or rather two girls whom I guessed must be Priscilla and Ruth because of the possessive way they flung their suitcases on the empty beds and the curious way they regarded me.

'Well, dears, have you had a nice holiday?' Mrs Green asked timidly. She looked rather frightened of them.

'Lousy, my brother had measles.'

'Lovely, we went to six theatres,' they answered simultaneously.

'Well, Priscilla and Ruth, this is Helen. She is to be your new dormitory mate. Brenda has gone up to Peverel. I want you to be kind to Helen. Perhaps one of you could show her the school.'

Anyway she can't smell worse than Brenda,' said Ruth. Mrs Green pretended not to hear and bustled out of the room.

'Supposing,' said Priscilla when she had gone, 'that you go and show yourself the lavatory. Ruth and I haven't seen each other for a month and I want to talk to her.'

I went out and shut the door quickly to hide my ridiculous tears. Then I regained my courage. It was disgusting to speak to me like that. I opened the door again.

'Well, of all the beastly cheek! What is it now?'

'Where is the lavatory?'

'Go down the passage and use your nose to smell.'

I sat down on the seat and looked once more at Swanage Bay. It was calm and blue and peaceful. I opened the window and looked down at the garden. Should I climb out and escape? It was sheer wall with no pipes or creepers. Should I throw myself down?

There had been a new girl in one of my school stories who had tried to kill herself but had been rescued in time and become a heroine. All the girls who had been cruel to her were sorry and she had become the most popular girl in the school. I did not think that if I dashed myself to death on the rockery I should become a heroine. I doubted even if anyone would notice or care.

Downstairs a bell clanked. For two minutes the house was full of screaming and rushing, then silence again. I sat and gazed at the sea. It was quite dark now and the lights on the promenade twinkled. I fell asleep. When I woke up voices were singing:

> 'Jesu, again to thy dear Name we raise
> With one accord our evening hymn of praise.'

There was more rushing and screaming and this time footsteps in the passage. Someone tried the lavatory door.

'Who is in here?' a strange voice asked.

I was too frightened to answer.

'Tell me your name at once.'

Still I could not answer.

A new and sterner voice that I recognised as Miss Fleming's said, 'Open this door immediately!' It was impossible to answer now. 'She may have fainted,' a kinder voice said. I thought it must be Matron's.

'Nonsense. She is just being tiresome.'

'But who is in there?' someone else asked.

'It's the new girl from Salisbury. I noticed she was not at Prayers. Really Matron this is your responsibility. I told you to look after her. I hope for your sake nothing serious has happened. You would have to explain your neglect to the Court. Come along now, we will find Peters and have him break the door down.'

I heard them go downstairs. I was trapped now. I knew I had better do something, when they broke in, I could not just be sitting on the lavatory seat. Could I be praying? I knelt down tentatively. It looked unlikely. Could I have fainted? I lay down on the floor. But would they throw water? I would be sure to show I was not really in a faint. I hated cold water. I looked around desperately. My eyes found the lavatory chain. I wound it round my neck. I could pretend I had killed myself. It was very uncomfortable. I rested my legs on the lavatory seat. How hot it was. Why did no air come in from the window? I wished they would find me and I could go to bed. I went to sleep, or it seemed like sleep. . . .

'She's round now,' a voice said. 'Give her air.' Someone undid my liberty bodice. It was tight and I hated it. I had never worn one before.

'Give me the Sal Volatile, Matron.'

Miss Fleming, who looked more worried than stern, poured horrid liquid down my throat.

'It's nasty,' I said. 'I don't want it.'

'*You* don't want it!' exclaimed Miss Amy. 'Who cares what *you* want after the fright you have given us? You are a very wicked little girl. If I were Miss Fleming I should send you home tomorrow. A child who has it in her to try to do what you have tried to do is not fit to be with other children. . . .'

'Hush, Amy,' said Miss Fleming. 'We will speak of that in the morning. Meanwhile there must be no talking. Anyone who says a word will miss netball tomorrow.'

'Coo, Amy's in a bate,' said Priscilla as the door closed.

'Hush,' said Ruth, 'they are sure to be listening.'

They waited for the footsteps to die away then Priscilla said, 'I say, new girl, we didn't mean to be so beastly. I mean we didn't mean you to kill yourself.'

'But I didn't. . .' I began. The door on the other side of the room opened and a figure in pyjamas came in from Waverley.

'Which of you is Dorm-head?'

'I am,' said Priscilla.

'Then we must confer,' the messenger announced.

There was a great deal of whispering then Priscilla said, 'New girl, I forget what your name is, Waverley here sent to ask what your father does.'

'Well,' I said doubtfully, 'he plays golf and goes to the office. . . .'

'Stupid, they mean what is he.'

'I believe,' I said, 'that it begins with C.'

'Chancellor of the Exchequer, perhaps.'

Everybody laughed. I racked my brains desperately. Whenever I asked Daddy what he did he always said, 'Earn your bread and butter and little girls shouldn't ask big questions.'

'I know,' I said triumphantly. 'Chartered accountant.'

The Waverley messenger signed. 'You're lucky. Our new girls are sisters and when we asked them the old one said merchant and the young one draper. When we said which did they mean, did their father have a shop the older said no, not exactly, and the younger said he had three. Really I don't know what this school is coming to. Of course we shan't be able to speak to either of them and that's awkward, the younger one's bed is the nearest to the chamber.'

When she had gone Priscilla said had I got any sweets and I said yes, but Matron had taken them and she gave me a piece of coconut ice.

'You can give me some of yours tomorrow. What have you got?'

It was a long list beginning with treacle-toffee from Cook and ending with peppermint lumps from Fullers.

'Are your people rich?'

I said I did not know.

'How many bedrooms have you?'

I counted carefully: 'Eleven, no perhaps thirteen.'

'Counting the maids' rooms?'

'Yes.'

'And downstairs?'

I told her a hall, a drawing-room, Daddy's smoking room, a dining-room, a billiard-room. I hoped she would not ask anything more because to think about the house made me sad.

'Priscilla has a flat in London, and a house on the River,' said Ruth proudly.

'Shut up,' said Priscilla, 'the kid's all right. Leave her alone. It's not trade and the house sounds pretty decent. Unless of course, she's lying.'

'Shall we torture her?' Ruth asked helpfully.

'No, I am too sleepy tonight. We'll do that tomorrow if she is still here. Amy didn't sound as though she meant her to be.'

Blessing Amy I fell asleep to dreams of tortures and awoke to find her bending over me.

'She looks all right now.'

'Poor little love,' said a voice I knew to be Matron's.

'Really,' said Miss Amy's voice, 'I can see nothing poor or lovable about her. My sister says best to forget the whole affair, and of course it would not be fair to hold it against Helen, but I for one shall never come to like the child. I shall do my best, of course, and you know I never have favourites, but always at the back of my mind there will be the feeling that even supposing a normal child might feel driven to try to kill herself, no nicely brought-up one would attempt to do it in the lavatory.'

– 6 –

It wouldn't be so dreadful being lonely if you could only be lonely alone. Only Fieldend wouldn't let you be alone. Herding girls together was part of its technique. I learnt mine too. Terrified of large chintzy rooms in which no one ever spoke to me I found sanctuaries in lavatories, in boot cupboards, in the passage outside Mrs Green's room where the very air smelt human and where you could wait for hours pretending that you wanted a clean handkerchief and didn't know she was having tea with the staff downstairs.

Walks were worst. I grew to dread the sunshine. Here there was no escape or deception. We assembled on a small platform of crazy paving outside one of the front doors to be counted. This done we were passed through the front gate in couples. I used to envy the animals in the Ark who had always someone to walk with. I never had. This meant that I must wait till the very last and walk with the mistress or be apportioned by her to some otherwise happy couple if she already had a mistress with her. It was best on the days when walks were taken with Mademoiselle because her eyes were also red with crying and as I couldn't talk French or she English our woe had no voice save the clip clop of her Paris heels on the cobbles.

The worst mistresses were those who meant to be

kind. 'Come along now, girls,' they would urge, preparing to blow their whistle, 'who will walk with Helen? Is this the way Fieldend treats its new girls?' No one can wait long with an East wind in their face and a whistle in their mouth, so soon I'd be apportioned to the final couple. Waiting on the crazy paved platform for the mistress to come out I could hear my school mates urge each other: 'Don't let's be last. We'll have to have Her.'

Lessons were bliss in comparison but even so they weren't all I had hoped they'd be. By Fieldend standards I wasn't at all clever. At my former school we had done very little precise work, our minds being groomed as it were to receive knowledge as we grew older. We were taught by women with zest and degrees. No one at Fieldend had a degree and the only one who had zest (apart from a beautiful music mistress who didn't count for unmusical me) was an outsider called Mrs Frost who didn't arrive till later when she came to substitute the speaking of poetry for a horrid subject called elocution. Lacking degrees or zest the Fieldend mistresses relied on text books. In geography you did Tasmania one week and Wales the next week. Doing implied starting with the climate and physical features and ending with the religion. A whole country took about a page and a half which it was accepted that you learnt by heart. Careful counting of the numbers round the table in form (we worked round a table not at desks, this being part of Fieldend's campaign against being thought like a high school) would permit you to learn only one sentence. Sitting at the far end as I did I could pretty well count on being asked what was the chief religion of the natives. As religion was my hobby this suited me. I meant to be a missionary anyway, so I felt that they wouldn't keep it, and I liked to think that all the text books would have to be altered because of me.

History was taught much the same way, taking reigns instead of countries. English meant verbs which I couldn't do, or essays, for whichI felt I had an aptitude if only they didn't always have to be about what I'd done in the summer holidays, or which was the nicest ball game. This last was taught in all the forms except the top form by the games mistress. Her name was Miss Smith. She was small and erect with a blue-veined face and eyes like a sly terrier. She would interrupt lessons to the Fifth on Browning by saying, 'Now Joan, I long to be in the netball field as much as you do but as we can't let's try and give our minds to listening to Maud reciting the fifth stanza of "Grow old along with Me".'

Being put back from the Fourth to the Third (which was also the bottom) hurt. It was done by the Headmistress who sent for me to her pink chintz sanctum and said, 'Well my dear, your mother led us to believe you were a clever child. You're not. Or anyway not by our Fieldend standards. I am putting you back to the Third. Now you don't want to cry about that. What a silly child. We can't all be clever. But we can all be nice little girls. Run along to Matron for a handkerchief.'

The nicest thing about Fieldend was Prayers. (Well, Church too, but this happened too seldom to count.) Evening prayers were nicer because morning ended with Roll Call and were brisk. Roll Call meant that the Headmistress called our thirty-five Christian names and we replied severally 'Ici' until such time as she and Miss Amy inherited some money and went to Paris for the summer holidays, after which we replied 'Here'. Evening prayers were not brisk, had no Roll Call, just a nice sad hymn and a prayer that said 'Lighten our darkness we beseech thee O Lord and by Thy Great Mercy defend us from all perils and dangers of this night.' Praying it the darkness of my first term did lighten though I sometimes felt that it was odd that so many prayers should be dedicated to the abolition of burglars. The day seemed to be even fuller than the night of perils and dangers.

I liked sad hymns best, particularly the ones at Church which everyone sang kneeling. The ones about Blood. We didn't have many of these at the small tin church opposite, which served as chapel for Fieldend and for my brother's school and as church for those who were too lazy to walk across the Bay to the parish church. It was most militantly cheerful and healthy. Low, as I see now. Even so I managed to feel good in it. Not good perhaps but lulled and luscious. It didn't seem so ignominious to be lonely and unwanted when the daylight was shut out by bright stained glass and a young man with a pleasant voice read about someone who had been despised and rejected of all men, a man of sorrows and acquainted with grief. I knew very few true words then and I was shocked into ardour by the adequacy of the 'acquainted'. The church was horribly ugly. I doubt if I should think holy thoughts in it now. Everything in it was brazen from the polished eagle to the vases on the altar. It smelt of soap and umbrellas. You don't see or smell these things when you are in love and I was madly in love with a God made manifest in words.

I had a great need to be solemn. Church satisfied that need. Even the grown-ups with their ghastly flippancy could not spoil that, though directly we came out they tried to. We flung our prayer books into our lockers and went to Peveril Point for a good blow. Lunch was the best of the week and in the afternoon we wrote letters home which began 'My own darling precious Mummy'. Prefects had envelopes six inches long and mauve notepaper with deckle edges and their initials cut out like embroidery on sheets. It came in beautiful boxes from Bobbys of Bournemouth and there was an appropriately coloured piece of sealing wax stuck in the ribbon. They had bath salts too and talcum powder that they got through answering advertisements for samples and suppressing in their address the word school. Going late to the lavatory a junior could fill her nostrils with Heart of a Rose or Eastern Romance. Alas the sample craze was crushed before I ever became a senior because a boy at a neighbouring prep school contrived to get a Rolls Royce car brought down for a trial ride. We admired his handwriting and felt him a hero.

As the weeks passed, and they did pass though it was hard to believe they could, my unhappiness became habitual. I couldn't remember being happy. In a way that made it better. I began to get used to no one walking with me and to accept snubs as tributes to my personality as I suppose a much-kicked dog accepts kicks. I gave up expecting to be liked or tolerated. As for being the darling of the school or any of the things I'd dreamed of at home, that was forgotten. In my woe I had become a drab and dejected little girl and when one day Miss Amy dragged me to my dormitory and bade me look in the glass I wasn't at all surprised to see a creature with lank plaits and a running nose and red eyelids.

Priscilla and Ruth, while not rubbing in my unpopularity, found it very convenient. Directly Miss Fleming had bestowed her goodnight peck they climbed into one bed and began to tell each other stories. I loved stories and forgetting myself once begged, 'Oh go on, please go on,' after which I was sternly commanded to go under the bedclothes and block my ears up.

This was more than I could bear so I eavesdropped. One night I heard Ruth deplore that this term no one had done anything Really Awful. This gave me an idea. At the worst I would be noticed, at the next best liked, best of all I might be expelled. Filling the filler of my new fountain pen my mother had sent me from London with red ink I squirted it down the neck of Mademoiselle as she came in to give us a French lesson.

My pride in my act was immediately dispelled by the knowledge that (a) only a low cad would have done it to Mademoiselle who was miserable anyway and couldn't keep discipline, (b) it was particularly caddish of me when Mademoiselle had been as sympathetic as one can without language.

Anyway the poor thing rushed from the room in tears and the form surrounded me with whoops of joy. I had received a bungy (india rubber) in the shape of a man's face and one old and one new pencil as tribute by the time Mademoiselle returned and sent me to Miss Fleming who called me a silly girl and told me to learn 'To be or not to be' that afternoon instead of playing netball. Since I loathed netball this was pleasure. I have since come to feel grateful to Miss Fleming for always choosing Shakespeare's speeches as impositions.

From that time on everyone was wonderful to me. I grew nastier and nastier. Although the war was presumed to be over I led a campaign to the effect that

Mademoiselle was a spy and spent hours collecting torn-up letters out of the staff waste paper basket and piecing them together to prove it. The poor thing had endured enough of the English without me and one morning we found ourselves being taught French verbs by Miss Smith. I tortured myself with the thought that she was probably going to perish of poverty in an attic. Still it didn't stop me enjoying my new popularity.

The Rebellion of the Lower School was interrupted by the End of the World. On our way up the hill to netball we saw a man with a poster announcing that it would be on Tuesday week. 'Repent ye,' it said. How avidly we repented. If God had only kept his appointment there wouldn't have been an unregenerate soul in Fieldend under twelve. Repentance necessitated confession and many tears were caused by ex-sinners owning up in public to the wrongs they had done in private conversation. The greatest trouble was caused by the game of Truth which at this time swept the junior dormitories. The sorrows of Doris and Doreen, my fellow new girls in Waverley, were added to by queues of girls all wanting to confess that they had called them the commonest girls in the school.

It was hard to make out whether it was worse to confess or be confessed to. My new-found complacency was shaken when Ruth said, 'Last night when you were asleep Priscilla asked me in Truth what your best point was and I said I didn't think you had any. In looks I mean. I don't suppose you mind at all anyway if you are going to the mission field. Still I thought I ought to tell you.'

Ruth's own looks were guaranteed by the legend that once taking visitors round the school Miss Amy had discovered her at her prayers and had murmured,

'How like the Infant Samuel.' A spiteful Waverleyite had suggested that this meant Ruth looked Jewish but Priscilla, ever loyal, had found a picture of Samuel in her Bible and he had golden hair cut in a bob very much like Ruth's. Priscilla had curly yellow hair which had already been hailed on arithmetic paper by a prefect from Derrington as 'liquid sunshine'. The note had been found in a hollow elm on the netball field by a senior who used it to hide her stays while she played.

Confessions lasted for five out of the ten days. As the dreadful dawn drew near (we were undecided whether the world would end at sunrise or sunset) we felt that something else should be done. Priscilla filled her brown knickers with fir cones and planned to sit on them all day but after a morning's mortification was caught by Miss Amy on the way up from lunch and accused of secreting food for a midnight feast in the dormitory. Taking down her knickers in Miss Amy's pink bedroom she was proud to glimpse in the long glass three red scars. Miss Amy, she reported, had looked pretty fierce at first, but when she heard the full story had said that Priscilla was a silly little girl, more sinned against than sinning, and had even dabbed some lavender talcum powder on the scars. We all agreed it was lucky it had been Priscilla because her mother was titled and lived near and her very fair hair and the title made her a show-piece when visitors came.

We were concerned about what to do on the world's last night. Peveril dormitory had decided to martyr its prefect, a lank girl called Monica who always cried if you drew back her cubicle curtain while she was dressing. It was thought to tie her to the cubicle rail by her long hair and strip her clothes off. If she screamed they would beat her with a wire hair brush. Waverley favoured charity and having worked hard on Doreen and Doris's vowels for nights planned to make them members of the secret society of their dormitory and initiate them into its version of the facts of life.

'Anyway,' they said cheerfully, 'it's only for one night. Though it's to be hoped Doreen won't say Coo er.'

As for me I had been working on a sermon. I wrote it in the back of my rough arithmetic book and it was called 'Jesus died. Do we care?' I had planned to deliver it on the world's last night to Priscilla and Ruth if they would let me. (I had always been the clergyman in the church games at home and fancied myself at it.) I fancied the sermon too. Writing it at night in the lavatory by the long bathroom I thought of words so much quicker than I could write them that I began to think I was inspired. The sermon was aimed, like all good sermons, at worldliness and frivolity. It inveighed against the use of face powder, though I was worried about this because Priscilla had confessed in Truth that Lady le Mesurier used Java Rice and I knew that my own mother used papier poudre. But frivolity wasn't its only target. I began by saying what I knew sermons should say and ended by saying what I myself needed to say. Paradise, people tell us, is the dream of the old and tired. I wasn't tired and I was ten, but it was my dream too. I peopled it not with the glorious company of the apostles but with the poets who were dead. I didn't know much about them but I knew that they were my people. No one had liked them. They hadn't been smart or clever or a success. One I knew had been sent to prison. (I had found a mauve suede volume of the Wilde fairy stories when I went to tea with the wife of the school doctor who always made friends with new girls, and had been told not to touch that book it's by a dreadful man who was punished in prison.) Anyway I knew that I would like them and they would like me. The dead wouldn't say what a big girl I was or how sad I didn't take after my lovely mother. They wouldn't tell me to wipe my nose or correct my grammar. We should have solemn talks about things that counted. Among the dead would be a melancholy young man who would like me especially because I had always understood him on earth and so few people had. He would be Jesus. Gazing out to sea from the lavatory seat I finished my sermon with a quotation from Tennyson about meeting my pilot face to face when I had crossed the bar. I had found it in a manual of devotion given to me by my rich godmother from Evesham. 'Pray every day whenever you brush your hair in your bedroom,' she had said, and, 'Never use sponges or flannels. Wash with your hands.' The old would be surprised if they knew how the young respond to their admonitions. I always knelt down every time I went to the dormitory (though I was terrified someone would see me) and I had flung away my horribly slimy flannel.

I wished the sermon looked as nice as it ought to look. Written in a soft pencil on the checks of my arithmetic book it looked awful. Only last week Miss Amy had observed in Scripture, 'I hear from Helen's mother that she is going to be a writer. Well she'll have to change her handwriting first.' Still it wouldn't matter how it looked when I declaimed it. I only hoped Priscilla and Ruth would be a willing congregation.

Surprisingly they thought it would be a very good idea. Now that Tuesday was getting so near they didn't much like it. The end of the world seems better when it's viewed from the week before last. We had sworn not to tell any day girls (who might blab at home like day girls do) or any seniors who would scoff, but Ruth had broken faith to a senior called Peggy who had got round her by reminding her that she had been her mother in the baby race at the sports last year. Peggy had laughed a lot and said that Juniors would think up anything. At the time (which was three days before) her laughter had been thought insulting. Now it was rather a comfort. Everyone's morale was low. Priscilla even threatened to tell her mother when she went home to lunch on Sunday. She felt that she ought to be warned to stop using the powder.

Why not, Ruth suggested, invite Waverley too and Peveril when they had finished martyring Monica. We could have hymns too then and there was a girl called Nora in Peveril who was good at playing on a comb, having been gifted by Heaven with the right amount of spit. The thought of so large a congregation made me lose my confidence. I kept titivating the sermon. I was bending over it in bed before lights out when Mrs Green confiscated it because it was written in a lesson book. After Roll Call at the end of Prayers the next morning Miss Fleming said, 'Helen Fletcher will come to me at once.' I wasn't sure whether to be pleased or afraid when I saw it on her desk. I comforted myself with thoughts of the Early Christians. After all I couldn't be put in a dungeon because the school hadn't got anything worse than a sick room and I couldn't be thrown to lions because its only animal was Miss Amy's scottie.

Miss Fleming picked up my rough arithmetic book distastefully. 'Well,' she said, 'no doubt you think you are a very clever little girl.'

I knew I ought to say 'No' but I couldn't say

anything. Turning to the end she read out what had seemed to me once to be a beautiful sentence. 'I am going,' she said, 'to talk to you as though you were much older. I am not used to little girls of ten who write long sermons about death. Especially little girls who bite their nails and forget to blow their noses. If it were one of the other juniors I would say it was just a phase. With you it's something different. Something nasty and unhealthy. I don't want to distress your mother, whom I like, by expelling you but I don't think you are fit to mix with other normal children. I have told Mrs Green to move your bed clothes to the sick room. You can stay there for the last three days of term. I will ask the Vicar to come and speak to you. He will tell you the difference between clean healthy Christianity and this unhealthy non-sense.'

The Vicar came that afternoon. He was very old and didn't seem so cross as Miss Fleming. I told him about the junior school and the end of the world and he smiled and said he wished we were right and that it were really coming. He explained that the Early Christians also had waited. Then he said the bit he had been told to say about religion not being a matter for little girls and how it was my duty to work hard and play hard. After that he made me kneel down and pray with him and as he shook hands held my chillblainy one for a long time and said, 'Poor child, what will they do to you here?'

I thought he meant would they torture me but next morning I was told to go down to breakfast as usual. The doctor's daughter had smuggled a white mouse into Prayers, and it wasn't till Break that I remembered that we all ought not to be eating biscuits or drinking milk, that we ought not to be here at all, because the world should have ended.

– 7 –

Back in Salisbury for the holidays, Ronald and I discovered that though we had come to like each other more than we ever had, no one liked us. Our mother felt that she had sent away two nicely brought-up children and had been returned two barbarians.

'That's more like my darlings,' she said hopefully when we had been bathed and shampooed and taken out of what she now called our odious uniforms. But the resemblance was superficial. We had entered into that state of prep school barbarism. Adults disliked us, we disliked adults. For several years we should have no contact with civilisation.

For one thing there was the problem of language. Ronald and I could understand each other but no one could understand us. Our mother even said we had picked up accents. She and Winifred, the housemaid, seemed surprised as they washed our hair that we hadn't also picked up lice.

Then there were the jokes. As long as we could remember there had been a print in the dining room called *A View of the River Po in Italy*. The first breakfast at home my brother noticed it and chanted, 'Look Hetch' (his new name for me) 'the River Po. Ho Ho what's a po?' The indecency reached my father behind his *Times*. 'How dare you, Sir,' he demanded.

It was the first time he'd ever said Sir to my brother. My mother hopefully offered us Teddy Tail of the *Daily Mail*.

Though we had longed for the holidays we couldn't settle. We mooched. We wouldn't stand up and we wouldn't sit down. We left the marks of our dirt on the drawing-room's walls. Even dressed in new holiday clothes and taken calling in the hired victoria we didn't remotely look like the children of the gentry.

Left alone we gorged. We spent our pocket money on whipped cream walnuts which we ate on the corrugated iron roof of the potting shed above Reeves' lavatory. Invited by him to go elsewhere while he emptied the earth bucket, we would munch and giggle.

I told my brother about Mademoiselle and he told me about his beating. He had received six strokes from the headmaster for walking down from football holding the hand of James Minor. There was no mention of this mysterious and terrible episode in his report which had the usual sprinkling of Fair and Very Fair leading up to Good for Nature Study (the last all the more benevolent since Ronald maintained he had never been taught any). As for mine it had three Poors and the only Good was for Mythology which was taught to the Sixth Form only. My character announced that I must try hard to settle down and be more like the other girls.

Apart from eating we enjoyed going to make faces at the German prisoners who were still behind bars although it was Peace. One hand in front of the nose meant go to hell, two meant go to hell and stay there. The wretched Germans seemed ignorant of our ill will and waved.

We had been uncomfortable for three months and

now comfort didn't suit us. We fled from our pretty nurseries, now turned into bed sitting rooms, to the mysterious cellars which Reeves used for storing pears and apples. The area that ran outside their windows along the front of the house was inhabited by millions of frogs whose croaking made the cellars even more like dungeons. The large loft reached by a ladder from the empty loose box we turned into a gymnasium (though we both hated gym) and inscribed over the entrance the motto 'Be prepared' though there seemed nothing to be prepared for now the war was over. It was almost a relief when I tripped over a rope and hurt my arm and had to be carried down the ladder by Reeves and taken in his arms (I wouldn't let anyone else touch me) to the Infirmary to be X-rayed. Matron was an old friend and in attendance herself, only when she came near she seemed to change to Miss Fleming. 'Don't cry,' she said, 'little ladies must be brave.' I fainted from pain and from the smell and because it seemed the easiest way out of being a lady.

It was nice being at home in bed and I lay propped up with a washed face and smoothed hair and an expression which I hoped resembled that of the noble and resigned Cousin Helen in *What Katy Did*. Ours was a fine house to be ill in. Ben was allowed to lie beside me and every time my mother went shopping she brought more books on what she called 'appro' which meant I read them and we returned them. I didn't have to pretend to be a schoolgirl any more and made Winifred rescue my beloved Tiny Tim, the bear with one ear and one leg, who had been thrust for three months in the dark corner of the drawer, and place him in bed beside me. I was once more my father's dear little girl and the last person he said goodbye to when he went to the office and the first person he greeted when he came in. I felt very proud when my mother said I must come downstairs because my brother adored me and fretted without me.

The dreadful thing about going back to school was not being able to tell anyone we didn't want to. To all the fond questions of Winifred, Cook, Reeves, the hired coachman, the people in the shops, we had replied, 'It's lovely.' Not even to one another would we admit how we hated it and how terrified we were of going back to it. The sight of the trunks was too horrible to bear and we took Ben across the fields to Old Sarum. It was the first of May. The sun shone and as we walked where the Romans had walked our feet seemed to bounce from the springing turf so that our heads came near to the blue heavens. There were harebells and an orange flower we called eggs and bacon. We sat on warm chalk and I died, but I didn't grow cold. I and the world grew still. Time wasn't, school wasn't. I thought eternity was a blue and beautiful word. Ronald said, 'Do you do Latin? James Minor does and he says it's frightful!'

I hadn't expected summer to come to Fieldend. There seemed no room. But it did. It crept in the cracks of the mock-mullion windows. You could smell it among the too bright flowers in Miss Amy's garden when you went to spread your bathing dress to dry on the lawn. I thought it was summer that did such odd things to me. I felt at once too near and too far away. Too near to myself and too far away from everyone else. The nearness made my breasts smart, the far awayness made me want to touch the chest of drawers before I went to sleep to prove it real. I felt that if I could only be alone I should discover a beautiful secret, and I lay awake at night pressing my eyelids apart with my fingers multiplying the minutes I could be alone.

Life became full of strange fears. I had to be along the long corridor and have one foot on the top stair by the time the lavatory plug had stopped pulling. I made myself say morning as well as evening prayers which meant tearing up to the dormitory before anyone else arrived after breakfast to make their beds. The prayers could be said as quickly as possible but to leave out one word was cheating. I felt that if anyone came in while I was kneeling I'd die of mortification. But I was far more afraid of breaking the magic by not saying them.

The fear of the lavatory chain brought a friend. One day in Break a Jersey cow girl called Brenda admitted in truth to fearing it too. In French after Break she passed me a note saying 'Will you be my best friend?' Hitherto I hadn't liked her. She had pale brown eyes and fuzzy hair which she did back in a slide as though she were already a flapper, and her hands were long-fingered and looked as though milk ran through them instead of blood. She couldn't bear ink on them and could always be found in the cloak-room rubbing them with pumice stone. She was tall and what Matron called 'big for her age', which meant that already she had been bullied into wearing a lace bust bodice for netball. Her father was a solicitor in Enfield and she talked a lot about his office and about their large house. Although she was always saying it was disgusting of Fieldend to let in Doreen and Doris she would cock one long white finger when she drank tea and often said 'ever so' and sometimes 'fore-head'. I hadn't ever been conscious of these things till she was my best friend but now I felt it my duty not only to be conscious of them but to like them and to incorporate as much as I could of them into my own behaviour.

You have to like your friends and if you can't like them you must love them. Loving Brenda was easier. You can accept almost anything in a goddess. I did my best all that summer term to transport Brenda to a heavenly plane. We walked together, shared a bathing hut together, sat next to each other in class and church and prayers and petitioned Matron to let us sleep together. This last was vetoed by Miss Fleming who said that she never liked girls who liked each other sharing the same dormitory.

'But Ruth and Priscilla. . .' I said.

'Are different,' replied Miss Fleming. 'They are nice sensible children. Besides, their families know each other.'

Obviously the thing to do would be to bring mine and Brenda's together at the Sports. My father wouldn't be able to come to them because the week before he had attended my brother's and had sprained a tendon running round the course with Ronald in the hundred yards and two hundred and twenty shouting, 'Come on, Sir.' He needn't have bothered. My brother won every race naturally and laconically. Heaven help my father, my mother said, since next year there would be the quarter mile. I asked my brother if it made him run any quicker but he said he hadn't noticed. He was the only boy at Derrington to win the Junior Sports Cup his second term.

'Isn't he a darling?' all the mothers said when he went up to take it from Priscilla's mother, Lady le Mesurier, who was giving away the prizes.

'The dear child,' she said patting his fair head. 'One would say a young Greek god.'

Our sports were rather an anti-climax. I didn't win anything, not even the Baby race. At least Brenda had the luck to be in the winning relay team so she went up for a prize. I pointed out that it was only luck since her team had had Ruth in and Ruth ran so fast that whichever team she was in always won the relay. Pinning her rosette on to her dress she told me not to be unsporting because I hadn't won anything. Success seemed to have gone to her head.

'Anyway,' I said, 'I don't want to be athletic when I grow up, I want to be clever.'

'Miss Fleming says you are backward.'

'Miss Fleming doesn't know everything. Anyway she isn't literate.'

'You mean literary. And you aren't either or you wouldn't like *The Garden of Allah* better than *The Last of the Mohicans*.'

I had managed to subtract *The Garden of Allah* unnoticed from the shelf in the staff room.

'At least,' I said spitefully, 'being literary doesn't spoil your figure like being athletic. Look at Miss Gilbert.'

Miss Gilbert taught Gym and had had a sonnet about Friendship in the school magazine, a most horrible sonnet which made being fond of someone sound like climbing crags or doing exercises on parallel bars. She had a bust which protruded aggressively and she held her stomach in so strongly that it came out at the back as buttocks. If you touched her in passing you sprang off like a ball from a tennis racquet. She deplored the wearing of stays and often began her lessons by saying, 'Now girls. . . stomachs in. How I wish I could have you all naked.'

She didn't like me, partly because I never held my

stomach in and partly because Brenda and I had stood outside the Studio where we did our Gym watching her performing in the staff lavatory which was visible through its open window.

'I saw you,' she said, springing along through the red currant bushes. 'I must say that if I hadn't met your mother, Helen, I'd say she was not a lady.'

'Well, here you are, darling,' said my mother. 'Couldn't you get your brother another ice? And Babs would like some more of that nice cake with strawberries in it. I must ask Mrs Dennis for the recipe.' It was typical of my mother to know the name of the school cook.

'Mummy,' I said desperately, 'this is Brenda.'

'So you are the little girl we hear so much about. Well, I hope you will knock some sense into my Helen. Run along, darling. Don't keep Babs waiting for her cake. You used to have such nice manners. I must speak to Miss Fleming.'

I gave Babs a glower. As I left I heard her saying, 'Is she really so much fatter round the top, Kitty, or is it that dreadful uniform? It's extraordinary you should have such a clumsy girl.' I made up my mind to ask her as publicly as possible about her chances of marriage. Still, it was awful being called clumsy and fat in front of Brenda. Looking back in my queue for ice cream under the elm I hoped the strawberry cake would be finished. They looked as though they were all talking about me and Brenda didn't look as though she were being especially loyal to me. One day, I thought, I'll show them. I'll come back married to the Prince of Wales.

When I got back Brenda's family had come up and had been introduced to Mummy and Babs. Though they were talking about their sons in the purring way mothers do talk about their sons when they were with their daughters I could see all was not going well. Mrs Bradley called Brenda 'Mummy's Girlie' and referred to her husband as Mr Bradley. When they had gone to have a word with dear Miss Fleming about their little girlie my Mother said, 'What did you say he did?'

'He's a solicitor.'

'Are you sure you don't mean an estate agent?'

'Mummy,' I said desperately, 'Do you think you could ask them to tea?'

'I don't see how if they live in Enfield.'

'No, I mean here. At the Grosvenor. They are staying there too.'

'But don't you think it would be kinder to ask some little girl whose parents are not down? What about that one over there.'

My mother signalled to Miranda who had ringlets down to her shoulders and parents who lived in the South of France. 'Won't you come out with my Helen tomorrow, my dear, or are your parents here?'

It was obvious that Miranda had manners too. At the end of the interview she was coming for the whole of Sunday and probably for some of the holidays too. And I was to be finished in Paris. I felt miserable about Sunday because Brenda hated Miranda.

Half terms were things you looked forward to for weeks and then felt to be a mistake. There was that unreal feeling of living at once in two worlds. The Grosvenor Hotel made a comfortable 'No-man's Land'. It was still more complicated by the fact that we had stayed there in the days before we went to school, in the period I now thought of as our childhood. Warm on its shingly beach I had written at eight my first literary work, four lines of carefully pencilled writing on a huge piece of foolscap purchased specially for that purpose. Their title, 'Revelations of an Old Salt', indicated that they were to be continued, but they never were. They looked so tedious written on the shiny lined paper and when I had composed them in the fisherman's boat they felt beautiful.

Then there was the torture-pleasure of rowing backwards and forwards in the dark green waters under the pier. If anyone ran along it the creaking made being underneath even more frightening.

And last and best there was the collection of sea creatures we kept in an old tub in what we called our secret passage, which was really a tunnelled stone staircase from the beach to the hotel terrace. On the terrace your mother would be making grown-up talk to other ladies and gentlemen in deck chairs, while a few yards away prone on your stomach you provoked a crab to walk past a sea anemone or tickled a tame shrimp with seaweed. Part of the magic of the sea creatures was that they couldn't be taken home, life in Salisbury being for them too inland. So you bade them farewell on the last morning of the holidays, feeling like God.

Breakfast the morning after the sports was unusual, consisting of cakes made out of bananas and the remains of the strawberries and cream. Then there was Church, to which dutiful parents came too; then we were free.

'Please God, let her be all right. Don't let her hate them,' I prayed tumultuously through the Te Deum. I decided that the last hymn would be a sign. If it were my favourite 'And now dear Father mindful of the love' it would mean that Mummy and Brenda's mother would get on quite well. I liked 'And now dear Father' very much, especially the verse about 'And now for those our dearest and our best'. Only I wished it did not have to tail off so badly into that moralistic couplet about perseverance. Hymns had a habit of letting one down.

The last hymn that morning turned out to be 'Father of Heaven whose love profound' which seemed a fairly good omen. It was soft and rolling and gentle and I liked it. The worst omen would have been one of those chirpy ones about soldiers.

Whatever happened I felt Ronald would be a comfort and I gazed at him admiringly as he led the Derrington choir out singing loyally. Ronald sang in church in the same easy way that he ran at sports. He carolled. If only his voice held off breaking, my mother said, the public schools would be quarrelling over him.

My mother had come to Church dressed in black corded silk and her skunks (the one with little tails but no muff). She always felt the cold in churches. Babs, arrayed in a navy coat frock my mother had ordered last summer and in the grey squirrel my mother had given her, looked passable or anyway much nicer than she was. Lady le Mesurier had on a black crêpe de chine dress and her inevitable leopard skin which looked as though it had been taken up off the hearth, my mother said. I thought it didn't matter because Lady le Mesurier looked as though she didn't mind even if it had been taken up off the hearth. I thought she would never mind what anyone said or thought of her, whereas my mother was forever asking, 'Did so and so ask after me? What did they say?'

By craning my neck impiously and risking a slap on the shoulder from Miss Smith who was in charge of

Church that day (you felt she had brought her whistle with her to blow in the Creed when it was time to turn round) I could glimpse Brenda's mother. She wore a reddish fur over a wine-coloured gown. I redoubled my prayers.

When we came out I felt so sick with caring that I almost ceased to care. The small tin church stood opposite the school and beside my brother's school. We were at the top of the town and across the roofs of residences mysteriously marked 'En Pension' you could see the sea. I played a kind of touch wood game with it. As long as my eyes could reach it I was all right. It was my friend.

I gazed at it now while my mother prodded the pavement with her silver-buckled shoe as she talked to Miss Fleming. Other people's parents came and went with their right quota of girls, 'your own dear Maud and poor Petronella whose parents can't come down because her brother is in quarantine, most kind of you to take her', and Miss Fleming bade them goodbye but she still went on talking to my mother. What could they be saying? I asked Babs if she knew but she said no doubt I had been making a fool of myself and went on raking at her face with papier poudre. Brenda came across and announced that her party were going to take a picnic to the Blue Pool but would be coming back to the Grosvenor for tea.

At last my mother beckoned to me and I went across to them. 'I was telling your mother that you are a very lucky little girl,' said Miss Fleming.

There must be an answer but it couldn't be 'Why?'

'Helen, Miss Fleming is speaking to you.'

'Lucky to have such a mother. Not many little girls are so well cared for. Your mother thinks of everything for your welfare. Deportment, dancing, riding lessons, and now extra elocution. You ought to be very grateful.'

'What,' I asked, 'is elocution?'

'You see,' my mother interrupted, 'she mumbles. Elocution is a lesson that teaches you to open your mouth and speak clearly. I can't think why she talks like this. Her father doesn't, I don't, and as you know her brother has a voice like a mountain bell.'

'I daresay,' said Miss Fleming grimly, 'that there is more in it than we know. Helen will learn to open her mouth when she learns to open her mind. At Fieldend we like our girls to be simple, natural and honest. Mind you they cannot all be pretty, one would not want them all to be clever. . . .'

'How true, how very true,' said my mother.

'But,' continued Miss Fleming, 'we like to think of them whatever their sphere in life' (you could guess by her voice that no Fieldender should ever be less than a vicereine) 'as good wives.'

'Well,' said my mother, 'unless someone I know gets some of her silly ideas out of her head and learns to blow her nose and stand up properly and answer when she is spoken to it's unlikely she'll ever get any husband at all.'

The best thing about half term was food. Even the terror of the new torture called elocution couldn't take that pleasure away from me. My mother had a headache after lunch and retired to her room with Babs, eau de cologne and a *Cachet faivre* borrowed from Mrs Brill who kept the hotel.

'Ah Mrs Fletcher I always say you are too good. No wonder you wear yourself out. I always say to Mr Brill that if there were more people in the world like Mrs

Fletcher it would be a better place.'

'Yes, I am kind,' said my mother. 'I don't suppose there's any special virtue in it. I was born like it. People just naturally love me. It's a gift I suppose.'

'I hope your daughter will take after you.'

'I am afraid that is not very likely. Helen has other interests. Come Babs, my poor head. . . .'

Ronald and I escaped to a boat. I felt thankful that Miranda had been prevented from coming by the arrival of a handsome uncle from Knightsbridge. Ronald disappointingly thought this a pity if she were pretty. We were not allowed to row beyond the end of the pier, but if you lay on the bottom like Christ in the story and looked at the sky you might as well have floated in the Pacific. I was so happy I wished I knew some poetry to say but all we had been learning was something about 'De Bruce thy sacriligious blow hath at God's altar slain the foe'. That didn't fit so I tried hymns, and they didn't either. Someday, I thought, I'll write my own poems. Not now. I am too lazy.

My mother's rest had mellowed her and when the Bradleys came in from their picnic to a late tea she was quite ready to talk to them. As I listened I marvelled at grown-up conversation. Brought in for no apparent reason, Winifred became my mother's personal maid, Reeves our head gardener, the Countess of Pembroke, with whom my mother had a slight acquaintance due to bowing at dancing classes, her greatest woman friend.

Perhaps Ronald and I looked surprised, so she stopped short and asked Brenda, 'And what, my dear, are you going to do when you grow up?'

'I hope I shall get married,' said Brenda.

'I am afraid,' said Mrs Bradley, 'my girlie is just a

home girl.'

'Then thank God for it,' said my mother.

'That's what her Daddy says. Mr Bradley doesn't hold with girls wanting to do things.'

My mother seemed to have had enough of Mr Bradley. She turned to Brenda.

'Well try and knock some sense into my Helen's head. She thinks more of you than of me.'

Could a goddess smirk? I found myself looking at Brenda for the first time with distaste.

Going up to school in the hotel car she told me she had had a lovely idea at the Blue Pool. We should try and be confirmed at the same time like brides. She had talked it over with her mother and the only trouble was that we should have to wear caps like nurses instead of lace veils because the Bishop of Salisbury was stuffy. Still, Brenda averred, you could do a lot with transparent sleeves and we'd look lovely kneeling together in snowy white.

– 8 –

Elocution proved, as I had guessed, a new torture. Only eight of us took it, and it took place in the gymnasium under the guidance of Miss Gilbert. I was always uneasy in the gymnasium which was associated for me with bars which I could get on but never off. Now it was necessary to walk eight paces towards the bars, briskly but gracefully, and to render in calm modulated tones a little piece by Ella Wheeler Wilcox or Sir Walter Scott, two poets for whom Miss Gilbert felt equal affection.

It was understood that whereas the other seven girls took elocution for pleasure and culture I took it to cure my mumbling which had already grown into speech defect. Miss Gilbert found it an excellent opportunity for curing my faults of posture too. One Tuesday I would be imitated by her taking my eight paces like a crab and the next like a fat man with my stomach stuck out.

But the classes were not so bad as playing to Miss Fleming. This odious entertainment took place at least twice a term. The school assembled at one end of the mock Tudor hall, the staff at the other. The piano was placed opposite the staff. You left your seat, walked up the middle of the room, announced the title of your piece and began to play. When the agony was over you bowed to the staff and listened politely to their comments.

In spite of my family's passion for singing and my brother's talents I had no feeling for music. Practising *Clair de Lune* at seven-thirty in the morning hurt my chilblains and I was glad when the pretty local draper's daughter who taught music declared it to be more honest to my parents if I gave it up. My two attempts of playing to Miss Fleming had been disastrous. In the first I had lost my place in *Down on the Farm* and burst into tears, in the second I had forgotten to bow to the staff and been fetched back again. I was appalled to learn that the elocution class was to recite to Miss Fleming as well as, or instead of, playing.

Miss Gilbert had a talent for the unsuitable and selected for my piece a nursery verse entitled 'The n'Ugly Little Man'. It might perhaps have been pretty recited by a child of six with golden curls. As I was eleven and had no curls I felt it unsuitable and resented the baby voice I was told to say it in. When halfway through Miss Fleming stopped me and asked, 'Isn't Helen a little big for this sort of thing?' I felt on her side for once. If only her observation hadn't seemed so funny to the rest of the school.

I was indeed too big not only for 'The n'Ugly Little Man' but for my age. Matron had already approached me with a bust bodice (sure sign at Fieldend of childhood left behind) and when we took our morning run after breakfast round the Point and back I felt uncomfortable. My portliness was the joke of the dormitory. Looking at the breasts of a prefect called Molly who threatened to be what the shop advertisement of that time called 'a Juno woman' I prayed God to let me stop growing.

My mother wrote to tell me that a woman friend of hers called Gwen (we were permitted to call her woman friends by their Christian names as a mark of modernity and an avoidance of the vulgarity of Auntie) had asked me to go to London for a weekend of the holidays. She had a small boy who often stayed with us with his nurse and I suppose she thought to return some of our hospitality.

What I knew of London I had learnt from books and advertisements. I believed implicitly in the carpet which posters depicted stretching up Ludgate Hill to St Paul's. I judged too from watching Winifred pack for my mother's weekends there that the citizens wore ball gowns with no backs to them and enormous hats with plumes. It was a disappointment to find life going on in Notting Hill Gate very much as it did in Salisbury, save that I walked with Peter and his nurse in Kensington Gardens instead of round Old Sarum. I do not remember having any intelligent reactions to any famous monuments I may have been shown.

As I undressed and climbed into my bed in the divan that had been made up for me in the dining-room (Gwen lived in a small flat) I found that my clothes were blood-stained. Too frightened to tell anyone I hid them under a cushion of a chair and fled to the lavatory. Investigation confirmed that I was the victim of a terrible scourge. God had selected me for particular and horrible punishment. I felt that whatever happens no one must find out and that somehow or other I must get back to Salisbury and perish in secret in my own home.

I put my pillow underneath me and slept somehow. When Gwen woke me to catch the early train I explained that my nose had bled and told her truly that it had done so often last term.

I had always known I was not like other people, now I had proof. It seemed to me that death was certain, but I dreaded the shame that must come first with my inevitable exposure. I wondered as the train sped home to Salisbury if my mother and Miss Fleming and Babs and all the people who had said I was not like other children had known that this would happen. I wondered if they would be pleased at my downfall. When the fat guard came in to ask, 'Are you all right, little Missie?' I could have cried. He wouldn't have come in if he had known, even though Gwen had given him half-a-crown at Waterloo. I couldn't think of anyone who would speak to me once they knew. Or only Ben; but then animals never turned against you whatever you had done.

I tried to pray, but it seemed futile. Obviously God had turned against me. I had thought him on my side but He was really on my mother's and Miss Fleming's. It was a dereliction I could not face. Perhaps this was what Jesus had meant when he said, 'Why has thou forsaken me?' Perhaps there was another Kingdom besides the Kingdom of Heaven. If I jumped out of the window would I find it down that chalk lane across that Wiltshire down? Was it buried beneath Old Sarum or hidden behind the looking-glass like the world of Alice? I knew that it was somewhere and that the people I loved belonged to it; Jesus and Lucifer and Ben and all my most loved animals and Keats and Shelley whom I knew nothing about but surmised to be on my side. No one in my kingdom would say 'Stand up and put your tummy in' or 'Pull yourself together'. No one would play games with balls. Everyone would be very beautiful and very serious and speak in quiet solemn voices.

The train and the fields brought their own peace. I took out my diary and wrote under 6 August 'Go home. And the herald of the Kingdom of Heaven shall be a child riding naked on a tiger down the Portobello Road.' I didn't know what it meant but perhaps it was a revelation.

Summer was all over Salisbury station. Heat on the platforms and the tunnels between them hollow and cool. We liked to race up and down them calling to each other but as I ran after Ronald when I had kissed my mother I realised that my legs couldn't run because something inside me that had nothing to do with them had grown old.

The horsehair seat of the hired carriage was hot again at the back of my knees. Outside my father's office in Fisherton Street the cool river tumbled. We must pick up a chicken from Mr Wright's the fishmonger's and some cakes at the Goldfish tea rooms.

'There is Lady Hunter, children, bow.'

'I am going to die,' I said, and was engulfed in darkness and the scent of my mother's fresh linen and eau-de-cologne.

Winifred carried me upstairs and began to undress me. When she saw my stained clothes she called my mother who sent her for hot water and assured me that I had nothing to dread. . . .

'It's beautiful and holy and means you are going to be a woman like me and have children.'

'I don't want to be a woman like you. I want to be a boy like Ronald.'

'You'll feel very different now this has happened. Lie still while I telephone the doctor.'

On the stairs I could hear her saying to Winifred,

'After all Miss Helen is very big for her age.'

'Still it don't seem right at eleven and her such a child still,' said Winifred mournfully.

She was very good to me. I stayed in bed a week and became part of a feminine conspiracy of silence. Neither my father nor my brother must ever guess what was the matter with me.

'But Winifred, some men must have known sometime surely.'

'No, Miss Helen, only doctors.'

'You mean it happens to my mother every month and my father never finds out?'

'Your mother is a lady and doesn't let him.'

'I told Ben and he said he didn't mind at all.'

'Sometimes I think you like that great smelly dog more than any of us.'

'I'll tell you a secret, he isn't a great smelly dog, he's a magic prince of my secret kingdom. You have been so kind Winifred, if you like I'll let you into the kingdom too.'

'You won't be needing magic princes soon, Miss Helen. Now you are growing up Mr Right will come along. We'll be seeing you married like your mother and having children.'

'I won't ever marry anyone unless it's Ben.'

When the long hot holidays were over fresh problems arose. When I went back to school I was not to tell anyone what had happened to me or indeed speak of it to anyone except Matron or Miss Fleming. If I did I should be expelled.

Whereas my mother took the view that what had happened to me might happen to any female, Miss Fleming thought that the fact that it had happened at eleven was another proof of what she referred to as my unhealthiness. I was not, she said, childlike. I had ideas.

With any other child she would have said, 'Put her into the Peveril dormitory with the thirteen- and fourteen-year-olds.' With me she just didn't know. Could I be trusted not to talk?

My mother felt sure I could. She had, she said, told me that ladies never mentioned such things.

All the same, Miss Fleming thought Ivanhoe would be better.

I shuddered. Ivanhoe was a dormitory inhabited by three prefects. One would be moved into Peveril to keep order and I should have her bed.

My mother had brought me back an hour early to have a good talk to Miss Fleming about all this. I went up to Ivanhoe to see what it looked like. It had windows looking out across the sea and mauve cotton cubicle curtains. On the bed nearest the window was a mauve silk nightdress case in the shape of a rose. On the washstand half of the dressing table were bath salts and dusting powder labelled Heart of a Rose. Instead of the usual photographs of parents was a huge shiny portrait of a sulky-looking young man signed 'Your Tony'. I was amazed by such evidences of adulthood.

'What exactly do you think you are doing in here?' a girl asked.

'I was just having a look.'

'Well go and have a look in your own dormitory. We don't allow juniors in here.'

'But I have got to sleep here. Miss Fleming says so.'

'Why?'

'I don't know.'

'Don't tell lies. You must know. Miss Fleming wouldn't put a junior in a senior dormitory without a reason.'

'It's because of something that I mustn't talk about.'

'Is it because you are not playing games?'

The expression seemed god-sent.

'Yes,' I said.

'Good God. How old are you?'

'Eleven.'

'You ought to be in a circus. How sickening.'

'It is sickening.'

'Oh I don't mean sickening for you. I mean sickening for us. When one gets to be sixteen one doesn't want infants around.'

Horrid though she was I had at least to be grateful to Barbara (for that was her name) for a useful expression. When anyone asked what was wrong with me I learnt to reply, 'I am not playing games.' It sounded negative but dignified.

As for the prefects in my dormitory they learnt to ignore my presence except when I could serve them usefully. I went to bed an hour before they did and theoretically was asleep by the time they came up. Or anyway it was convenient for them to believe me asleep so that they could carry on fascinating adult conversations by moonlight.

Once the conversation concerned a female pet monkey belonging to Joyce, the other prefect's brother, which was said to have the same complaint as human females. I could bear it no longer.

'Do you mean it was "Not Playing Games"?' I asked from my pillow. For some reason the question rendered Barbara and Joyce almost human. Though they rebuked me sternly for listening to conversations not intended for me, they agreed I was a scream and their titbits of information made me more muddled than ever about what are now called the facts of life. The trouble was that there were so many other facts of more immediate importance. A new girl had come to the school bringing worldliness with her. Her mother was an actress, her father an editor of a weekly. They had bought a house outside Swanage and gave weekend parties to celebrities from London. Though I didn't really approve of Thelma I admired her background. Though she was bottom of everything except French which she spoke far too elegantly for Miss Smith, and couldn't play netball at all, she changed the tone of the middle school. Where others had spoken of boys, she spoke of men. She endured the weekly boredom of the Art class with a prefect's penniless uncle because she said men liked their women to know about Art. Plain, bespectacled and shaped like a pear, she would regard herself for hours before her looking-glass, seeing not the girl she was, but the woman she would be.

'I shan't be beautiful, Helen, but I shall be smart.' Smart meant for me black and white check and beautiful meant pale blue tulle, so I told her, 'I hate smart.'

'You won't be beautiful either,' she said, 'But perhaps you'll be clever.'

Netball that before her advent had been a torture now became fun. Being bad at it ourselves, we succeeded in making being good at it ridiculous. It became no longer the thing to have muddy knees. Thelma would ask to leave the field because her breast had collided with the goal post and, 'Games are all very well, Miss Smith, but a girl has to think of her womanhood.'

It had seemed shameful alone to be making starfish

on the parallel bars in gym and not to be able to get down. With Thelma it was funny. To Miss Gilbert's sarcastic enquiry about the size of our tummies Thelma would reply, 'My sister says voluptuousness is quite the thing.' Her sister was secretary to a film actress and was our goddess.

Mysteriously Miss Fleming was never so cross with Thelma as with me. Perhaps it was because her family were celebrities, perhaps because Thelma had a way with adults and I hadn't.

She had a technique of crying in rows till you felt her tears would burst her glasses.

'You don't have to cry like that, Thelma my dear.'

'Honestly Miss Fleming, I do. You say the school is just like the world and I am a failure at school, so I'll fail in the world.'

Her tears were in part sincere and often I would be fetched out of bed by Matron and told, 'Thelma is crying in the long bathroom and no one can get through to the lavatory.'

I don't know why I went since she wasn't my best friend. People thought of us as two oddities together and comforting Thelma might mean Sunday spent at that curious bare house where her parents lived and where it was useless to be shy because distinguished visitors expected one to take part in intellectual conversations.

I found that it was much easier to be friends with Thelma's mother's friends than with my mother's. They never said, 'Wasn't I big for my age' or 'Did I like school'. Sometimes they asked me what I thought about something important like God or Death, but mostly they told me about their love affairs which sounded sad and beautiful.

I never told my mother about the kindness of Thelma's mother because I felt sure she'd say we must have Thelma to stay in Salisbury and I felt confident our house would bore Thelma.

Elocution continued its peculiar torture until half term when Miss Gilbert suddenly disappeared with a nervous breakdown (had Thelma and I caused it?) and her place at gym was taken by Miss Smith and at elocution by an outsider called Mrs Frost.

She wore powder blue and was plump and had a face like a parrot. Her eyes were bright blue but not hard. We had all learnt 'The Old House by the Lindens' but she didn't seem to want to hear the eight of us repeat it. Instead she said, 'Tell me what you think about it.'

Brenda said, 'It's by Longfellow' and Mrs Frost said, 'Not what you know, but what you think.'

I said, 'I think it's a cool poem, cool and sad.'

She asked if I liked poetry and I said I didn't know much, only the Scott and Browning and Ella Wheeler Wilcox we'd been learning, so she spent the rest of the lesson reading 'In Memoriam' to us out of the copy of Tennyson which Miss Gilbert had kept to make us do 'She left the Web she left the loom' to music for the improvement of our vowel sounds. Her voice when she read the sad words was flat and expressionless, whereas Miss Gilbert's had always been full of expression. She told us to choose four stanzas to learn for homework, 'Four different stanzas. I do not like to be bored even by Tennyson.'

As I went out she called me back and gave me a battered book called *Poems of Today*. 'You can learn something out of this too.'

I learnt 'Nod' to say to her; and 'By a Bierside' to say

to myself because I liked it:

> Death drifts the brain with dust and soils the young
> limb's glory,
> Death makes justice a dream and strength a
> traveller's story.
> Death drives the lovely soul to wander under the sky.
> Death opens unknown doors. It is most grand to die.

She was very polite to everyone about their 'In Memoriam', only saying that they need not wave their hands about (Miss Gilbert had been a devil for gestures) because poetry didn't need gymnastics to help it. Everyone thought this a joke against Miss Gilbert and giggled. Then she asked me what I had chosen and I said 'Nod' and she said, 'A soft sleepy voice for "Nod", please.'

Suddenly I found myself with my back to the wall bars gabbling. She didn't stop me but at the end she said, 'Listen.'

I had never heard a poem read before by someone who cared for poetry and not ranting.

'Please read some more.'

What would you like?'

' "By a Bierside." '

'No, I think "Martha".'

At the end of the class she stopped me again.

'If you stay I will read you your "By a Bierside". I think perhaps it's rather private for the others.'

'That's why I didn't tell you I had learnt it.'

When she had read it she asked if I had learnt anything else and I told her how I had copied most of the ones I liked because I dreaded giving her the book back.

'I will send you a copy up from town tomorrow if

you promise me one thing. Learn the poems you love. Don't copy them down.'

Sure enough the book arrived the next day and was handed me by Miss Amy who read the inscription 'To Helen, may she continue to love poetry', and said that she hoped my head would not be turned by all this fuss.

Mrs Frost never turned my head. She awakened my intellect. The poems she taught me to find for myself made me come alive for myself. In a way they made me invulnerable. If I couldn't be sociable and pretty like my mother, or smart and witty like Thelma's mother, or a good school girl like Priscilla, or a sweet home girl like Brenda, I could be the me the poets spoke to. Mrs Frost never asked anything of me except my love for poetry. Gradually I overcame my shyness and so far forgot my mumbling as to say 'Let men not to the marriage of true minds' to Miss Fleming without noticing that she was there.

Miss Fleming found it even more unsuitable than 'The n'Ugly little Man' but found it hard to say so to Mrs Frost who backed up her opinion of me by putting me in for the Poetry Society examinations. All one had to do was to recite (or as Mrs Frost said 'speak') three stanzas of 'We are the music makers and we are the dreamers of dreams' and a poem of one's own choosing. The examiners had the Frost point of view about voice and gesture and success was easy. It was hers and not mine, but it served to silence Miss Fleming.

– 9 –

The holidays brought death and disruption. The death was Ben's. One day he seemed too tired and old to stand up (though he was only six months older than me hey assured me that for dogs you multiply by seven) and the next day my mother broke it to me that he had died in the night. I discovered from Reeves that the vet had come up and shot him. It was, they said, kinder. If loved him I should have wished it. But I would have wished to have known. He must have thought I knew and had betrayed him. He must have known when he aw the gun. I wished I had died with him; perhaps some of me had.

I locked myself in the spare room and wept all the morning, refusing to open the door. At last Reeves brought a ladder and carried me down in to the front garden. Since I wouldn't eat and lunch was long over he gave me tea out of his tin cup and bread and jam in he harness room. The tea tasted strange, but I never knew whether it was the tin or my tears. I wanted to bury Ben next to the horse in the vegetable garden, but apparently the vet had taken him.

As things were, Reeves said, it wouldn't matter any. It was the first hint I had that we were going away.

My parents had decided to move into a smaller house in a place called Broadstone. When he wasn't

working my father liked to be playing golf an
Broadstone had a first-class golf links. My mother, wh
found Salisbury stuffy, would find fresh life in nearb
Bournemouth.

Ronald liked golf and was philosophical. To me i
was the end of the world. Or anyway the end of wha
Ben's death had left of the world. Knowing I mus
leave them forever I began to see the beech trees on th
top of the chalk downs and the harebells and eggs an
bacon. I thought that part of me would stay foreve
where we had searched for secret passages at Ol
Sarum and in the dark green meadows called the Wate
Butts where we had fished with bottles for minnows.
had thought of these things as one thinks of the part
of one's body. It hadn't mattered that they wer
beautiful. Now, saying goodbye, I knew that they wer
and I knew that I should loathe Broadstone with it
sand and its pines.

It was, my parents said, very healthy. People came t
it to get well. Then I should go there to die. My mothe
said I should feel very different when I had been to th
thé dansant at the King's Hall in Bournemouth.

It's lucky Broadstone has a junction because at leas
that is something. Trains coming and going an
waiting for other trains at least make a centre in
town that hasn't a market and a village that hasn't
green. Red brick houses with gables had simply sprun
up everywhere, each with its quota of pines. On
pine looks much like another and one villa like anothe
and there was no way of telling the Major's house fron
the Colonel's. Most Broadstonians were one or th
other and many had been to India.

It ceased being a matter of who was gentry and wh
common and became merely a matter of who was

member of the Club which was, of course, the Golf Club. Till my parents found a house, we were to share one with a Major and Mrs Pugh. Apparently they had found themselves poor at the same time as we had found ourselves poor – poverty, I learned, as much as golf being the cause of our desertion of the Red House.

It soon became clear that not having a house of her own was to cost my mother more than having a house of her own. She liked the Pugh's house so little that she spent all her money getting out of it. We would set out every morning by car for Bournemouth and drink coffee in Smith's in the Square and go shopping in Bobby's till it was time to have lunch (a Dover sole and a banana split at Bright's) and go to the Westover to the pictures. When these were over you could either have tea and watch the roller skating there or walk along the road to the King's Hall *thé dansant*. Either way we knew nobody. It was all very different from Salisbury where we had known everybody.

Perhaps because she was bored with having no one but children to talk to, my mother made contact with the professonal dancers. There was a saturnine man with a pointed chin and pointed toes and a very dark and wicked-looking lady. My mother used to dance with the man and Ronald and I shared the lady, who bore up bravely. When there was a waltz they put out the lights and made stars and spots twirl from the ceiling. There was a man in the band who moaned, 'What'll I do when you are far away and I am blue, what'll I do?' most sadly.

It was very different from the dancing class at school or at Salisbury but as my mother said it passed the time away and if we hurried we should be back in Broadstone before Daddy's train came in. Whatever happened we were not to tell him where we had been. Perhaps my brother had better say he'd been practising his putts.

In fact the new life suited me very well. I had nothing to do but dream. I dreamed in the warm dark of the pictures, in the soft light of the King's Hall, and in the fierce dark of the open car on the journey home. In my dreams I grew up.

Broadstone's church was high. Enthusiasts, even golfers, called the Vicar Father; there was a Children's Corner and paintings of holy children with pink faces and bright yellow fringes. When you went in from the cold it smelt nice.

On Sunday morning there were two services, Matins at eleven and Choral Eucharist at ten fifteen. Since my father had to work in Salisbury all the week his Sunday golf was important. So too, in a different way, was his Sunday church. You couldn't get two rounds in and eat roast beef if you went at eleven, so we had to go at ten fifteen and make the best of it.

Ronald and I never knew where we were in our prayer books because we always seemed to be beginning in the middle of something. My mother was thwarted in her desire to sing hymns in her rich contralto. My father could never find the right place for his bass, manly amens. When in the sung creed we reached the bit about 'And was made incarnate of the Virgin Mary' and everyone else in the church knelt down, my father would whisper savagely, 'Stand up, children, or I shall take you out.' I shall never forget the look on his face on Palm Sunday when the suddenness of mass movement found him processing round the aisle with a palm in his hand.

Our parents' natural centre was the Golf Club. My

mother preferred it to the course. There was a ladies' lounge where you could sit by a gas fire and read *Britannia* and *Eve* and *Punch* and the *Tatler*, only you had to be ready to leap up from your comfortable chair when the ladies' captain, Miss Jackson, came in.

Miss Jackson had hair as short as my father's and wore man's clothes except for trousers. I suppose I should say except for plus fours because everything about her was dedicated to golf. If you saw her go up the aisle in church she still looked as though she carried her clubs on her shoulder (she disdained the effete who employed caddies). She lived with her sister Mrs Sampson, who was her softer version and ran to lace, in a bungalow among the pines by the Poole Road. The tragedy of her life was that you couldn't organise golf matches at night, so she gave parties for what she called Broadstone's young people and organised progressive games instead. Sometimes they were book teas and sometimes pencil and paper evenings. Either way I couldn't get out of them by saying I hated games because Miss Jackson would reply heartily: 'All the better, my dear, if you are clever.'

Even if I had been I feel my cleverness would have been the wrong kind. I had never read any of the books which people came disguised as (you pinned paper symbols on your breast) and both Ronald and I were sadly deficient in a sense of smell and couldn't distinguish ink from soot when blindfolded.

We were less embarrassed at the local hops in the Women's Institute Hall. These were divided into two kinds. The first, called Private Subscription, was got up by Miss Jackson for some charity and at it you could dance with anyone who asked you. The second, called just 'A dance', you went to either with your family and danced with Daddy and Ronald, or with a party and danced inside it. Once I broke the unwritten law and danced with Mr Shorto, the garage proprietor who wore Oxford bags; and once my father allowed me to break it to dance with the golf professional, Mr Corlette. Like the professional in Salisbury Mr Corlette was my father's chosen champion. He was an even better player, winning matches everywhere. There was absolutely no nonsense about him. He danced as well as he golfed and he had four pretty daughters who we longed to know, but who would never smile at us. Perhaps their taboo was as strong as ours.

My mother did better with the golf secretary who looked like Owen Nares and lived with his wife and twins of two in a small white villa called Chez-Nous. To the twins, as Mrs Smithells often said, she was a real fairy godmother. She bought them every sort of toy and gadget and in return I was allowed to help to bath them 'to bring out the woman in me'.

I liked animals very much better than babies and was determined never to have any. When I was twenty-one I should live on an uninhabited island and keep all the beasts who hated man.

My mother liked to find someone poor to patronise and this was a difficulty in Broadstone which really didn't have a working class. In a street behind the church (it was perhaps Broadstone's only street, the rest were straggling roads) in a semi-detached tall villa that must I now know have been quite twenty years older than any other house in the place, lived a sad family called Mann.

The mother was an invalid, the youngest sister Flossie an idiot, the house was kept going by Ida (aged forty) who did all the housework and made hats, and

Una who was said to be an actress in London. Ida had been an actress too till her mother had taken to a bath chair. Now there were two invalids to one bath chair and both needed to be pushed to church. Mrs Mann lived for the Vicar and poor Flossie seemed only happy when she smelt incense.

The Manns were just right for my mother. Their being genteel made it better. 'Chicken for dinner, Miss Mann does so enjoy it, poor dear,' she would tell the female half of our married couple. (We had moved far quicker than my father had intended, neither Mrs Pugh nor my mother having found the other quite-quite.) After dinner poor Ida would pay for her bit of breast and bread sauce by playing 'Because' and 'Parting long into the night'. Well, perhaps not the night. I never saw that in Broadstone, but at least till ten-thirty when my father would get out the car and drive her home.

Ida hated Broadstone and pined for theatrical lodgings in Earl's Court. If you took her to a theatre in Bournemouth she would dash into a dressing-room to see some old trouper she had played with and come back refreshed. Even the dreariest third-rate actress must have felt themselves a success when Ida gazed at them with awe.

To keep up her morale she wore stage make-up which in 1922 looked even odder than it would now. You would meet her pushing the drooling sister to church with her face decked to play Mrs Tanqueray. It was difficult not to stare at it because if you took your eyes off Ida you inevitably looked at Flossie and looking at Flossie was terrifying.

My mother's charity towards the Manns involved me involuntarily. I had mistakenly told her that I was supposed to learn some poems for Mrs Frost in the holidays. Ida, said my mother, should coach me and my father should pay. It would be a way of giving the poor proud things some money.

In vain did I insist that poetry meant something different to Mrs Frost and me than it did to Ida Mann. My mother was in love with the idea. I spent dreadful afternoons closeted in the Mann front room with the ex-actress and *The Reciter's Golden Treasury.*

First I had to do something for her that I had learnt for Mrs Frost last term and I did 'Nod'.

'Too quaint. A dear little piece. But you want to give it more life. Try and put in a gesture as though you saw the sheep coming over the hill.'

'Won't you do something?' I pleaded.

Ida let herself go with an epic about a little boy leaning over a staircase and watching a party. She seemed to delight in the couplet:

> 'Marbles would bounce on Mr Jones's bald head
> 'But I shan't try.'

It seemed to me that she put into it the suppressed coyness of forty years. For my piece for Mrs Frost she selected one by Ella Wheeler Wilcox which began:

> 'My dear, it isn't the big things, great deeds of valour and might
> 'That count the most in the summing up of life at the end of the day.
> 'But it is the doing of small things, small acts that are just and right
> 'And doing them over and over again no matter what people say.
> 'In smiling at Fate when you want to cry and in keeping at work when you want to play,
> 'Dear these are the things that count.'

I remember that I never put sufficient intimacy into the dears. I think it confirmed Ida's belief that I was a cold character, not at all like my wonderful mother.

Mrs Frost was very polite about what she must have thought an odd choice. Perhaps it wasn't a poem but it was, she supposed, sincere. When the others had gone I told her about Ida and about my new scheme that she should teach me literature. I had made my mother promise to pay for private classes if Mrs Frost would give them me. She said she would and that she would have a talk to Miss Fleming. I don't know what they said to one another but Miss Fleming told me that she hoped I didn't run away with the notion that I had literary talent just because Mrs Frost spoilt me.

'Your mother tells me that you fancy you are going to write. I had to tell her honestly that your essays show no talent whatsoever. They are untidy and unhealthy.'

The untidiness referred to my atrocious handwriting, the unhealthiness to my last week's essay which had horrified Miss Smith by its announcement that it would be wonderful to die, 'to fade upon the midnight with no pain' and meet Shelley and Keats in Heaven. It had been entitled 'Wishes' and had come as rather a shock, everyone else having wished for more virtues, better features or more netball. Miss Smith had put my book at the bottom of the pile of exercise books and given me five out of ten for it. Even Thelma had got six for wishing to go to the Fourth of June to see her new boyfriend.

'That, although undesirable is healthy,' said Miss Smith. 'As for Helen, if she does want to die that is morbid and if she doesn't to say she does is insincere.'

I dare say she was right, but it was horrid of her to say it in front of the class. I dare say Mrs Frost found the death wishes of adolescence trying too, but she had the tact to allow me to let Swinburne and Dowson express them.

I cannot read *The Forsaken Garden* now without seeing the green baize table-cloth of the staff-room table round which we sat while she taught me. I sat and clutched its bobbles in my hot hands. I don't know what I thought it meant, translated into terms of my private self, but I know it brought me ecstasy. I would kneel by the window in the staff lavatory at night when they were sure to be at supper and say it to myself. Once I had said my prayer there. Poetry was taking the place of religion.

Because of this I agreed with Brenda that we should be confirmed soon. If I waited much longer I thought I might lose my faith and perhaps our love. I had sent her *The Shropshire Lad* in mauve vellum with deckle edge pages in the holidays and she had responded with a tin of shortbread.

I was afraid she lived on a lower level.

Brenda and I were the only two candidates for confirmation so the Vicar said we must go to Eaton House to be prepared. Eaton House was a smaller school about three roads away. Fieldend despised it because it was bad at games (we were wonderful) and it took the daughters of local tradesmen as day girls. We only took the daughter of the Vicar and Doctor. I don't suppose Eaton House wanted us much either but they were very civil. Brenda and I felt like ambassadors to a minor state.

The Vicar was elderly and dreamy. On earth he had an invalid wife, a delicate daughter (at Fieldend) and no money. No wonder he preferred to live half in Heaven. I don't suppose he relished much making the Kingdom of Heaven attractive to adolescent schoolgirls but he was gentle with us. I felt ashamed of Brenda for asking about what material her veil could be made of the first time he asked for questions.

'Nuns' veiling, my dear.'

'But that's what nurses wear.'

'Nurses and nuns.'

'Lace would have looked so lovely.'

'It is your soul that God will be looking at. You are to be confirmed, not married.'

The mention of marriage gave our Eaton House colleagues an opportunity to titter. I felt ashamed of Brenda and I asked the trickiest question I could think of about Transubstantiation. On the way out the Vicar told me he'd lend me a book on the subject and added that it was as bad to be mentally vain as it was to be physically vain. 'Not all vanity has to do with lace veils, Helen.'

I felt ashamed of myself and more than ever conscious that I was being confirmed too late. I had never heard of the poems of Herbert (though I had been christened in his church at Bemerton) and my allegiance was divided between hymns and Swinburne and Shelley.

Miss Fleming didn't help. Her contribution to our feelings about confirmation was to warn us that we wouldn't feel any different. The good feeling would come after we had been faithful communicants for several years. No doubt she was right to warn us against disappointment but the God I had believed in so far was capable of coming into Swanage Parish Church and dragging Helen up to Heaven by her nuns'-veiling veil. He could and would do anything. Besides how could I be filled with the Holy Ghost and feel nothing? I felt about magic that wasn't magical much what I felt about the conjuror cutting the girl in half when adults assured me he hadn't done it. What could be the point of it?

Of course my parents were coming down and so were Brenda's. The posts brought various editions of *The Christian Year* which I put in the drawer with my handkerchiefs. I never read them because they didn't look like books that you were meant to read. My mother sent from Beale's in Bournemouth a jade green prayer book as big as a novel and made of shagreen. It had enormous print, almost as enormous as the handwriting of my mother who wished me the appropriate wishes for my soul on the mottled flyleaf. It was the first time she had ever seemed to recognise that I had one, and somehow the delayed recognition seemed an intrusion.

Even Mrs Frost was moved to suggest that we read *The Hounds of Heaven* instead of *Prometheus Unbound* at my private poetry lesson, but when I cried out half way, 'I hate it, I hate it!' she said perhaps we were both happier with Shelley.

My mother had produced the most unsuitable frock made of some stiff embroidered lace that came from Italy. It was so transparent that it had to have its own white silk slip, but the slip hadn't sleeves and so my arms showed through. This occasioned frantic telephone calls to the Vicarage, but was finally conceded. Apparently it was the nuns's veiling that the Bishop really minded about. If your head were decorously decked in it he didn't look at your body.

'I do think it's lovely,' Brenda said, looking at the

debated dress spread out on my bed. 'Do you think we can get away with a little powder? I've got a box hidden in my dancing stockings. Naturelle of course. It would make all the difference.'

'Do you think the Holy Ghost minds if it's naturelle or rachel?'

'I think you are horrid. What's more I don't think you ought to talk like that. It's probably blasphemous. I don't know what's come over you lately, but it's obvious you don't love me any more.'

'Well, that's true anyway. Fancy you having the sense to guess. I think you are horrible. Stupid and vain and common.'

'Your mother was right. You are a cruel unnatural girl. I always tried to stand up for you.'

'Well, are the Brides of Jesus falling out?' said Barbara coming in to brush her hair. 'Run along, Brenda, go and weep in your own dorm. We have enough adolescence here with Helen.'

Brenda never wept in vain. She cried so much that Matron was fetched and in turn fetched Miss Fleming. When the time came for our before-confirmation talk she told me that I should be ashamed of myself for being so unkind to Brenda.

'Not that I ever approve of these violent friendships. They are always unhealthy. One moment the school calls you David and Jonathan and the next you won't speak to each other. Your mother rang up about the time of the service and I told her about it. Really Helen, you are a most difficult girl. I don't know any child I have had such trouble with. You will apologise to Brenda. I hope you feel that all this makes you worthy of tomorrow's ceremony.'

Brenda was in Matron's room, lying down with

cotton wool on her eyelids. Her looks mustn't be spoilt for tomorrow. I had meant to say I was sorry, but when I saw her it all came up again and I said: 'Miss Fleming says to tell you I am sorry.'

She gave a little moan and said, 'Pass me Matron's lavender water.'

On Saturday nights we put on party dresses and danced after supper. I had a new dress of burnt orange chiffon. I disapproved of clothes and it embarrassed me that my mother always sent me such pretty ones. This evening I didn't mind so much as usual when the seniors came and told me it was charming. At supper I found an opened telegram on my plate (Miss Fleming always opened them in case of bad news). It read 'Miss Fleming has told me all about your trouble do not worry too much darling will be with you tomorrow all love Mummy.' It did not so much convey to me that my mother had become gifted with understanding as that she welcomed any rift with Brenda because it would mean she would no longer have to be civil to her common family. I looked in the glass and saw not only that I smiled but that my face wore a most worldly expression for a candidate for confirmation. Priscilla, who took stepdancing and would usually wince if asked to partner me, whisked me away to dance 'Last night in the back porch' so that she might find out what had happened between me and Brenda. She smelt much nicer than Brenda smelt and didn't breathe so heavily. Perhaps it wasn't the eve of confirmation I had pictured, but in its own way it was a triumph.

– 10 –

The Bishop seemed on the side of Miss Fleming. He welcomed our faith but doubted if it would last. The world held many perils. Few cleaved to the Church in these times.

I had had moments when I would have cleaved to the Church were I the last Christian on earth. The moments had passed. Perhaps it was that orthodoxy wouldn't tally with my dream world. I had sought God as a refuge from the grown-ups and now couldn't share Him with them. Still less did I wish them to share their God with me.

I could have wished too that it had been Priscilla and not Brenda who had knelt with me at the altar rails. But Priscilla, when asked by Miss Fleming whether she did not think it was time she was confirmed, had answered that she had not yet made up her mind.

'Isn't that rather a terrible thing for a girl to say, my dear?'

'I know, Miss Fleming, but wouldn't it be worse to act a lie?'

I had been shocked when rumour of this had reached me but now I didn't know. At least Priscilla wouldn't have Matron demanding whether she was going to Early Service in the same breath as she asked whether she had been to the lavatory or cleaned her teeth. Once my relationship with God had been my own affair now everyone took an interest in it.

Girls going to Communion met in the staff sitting room at 7.45 to drink a cup of tea and eat a biscuit. Thelma, whose mother was High, had warned me that if I did this it would spoil everything. I refused the cup of tea and so did she. We both fainted, Thelma at the beginning and I when for me it was over.

Next Sunday Miss Fleming came herself and insisted that everyone drank her tea. 'If you refuse, Thelma there will be nothing for it but Communion after Matins. I cannot let you injure your health. Besides you and Helen were a great nuisance last Sunday. Drink up your tea at once.'

Swallowing the tea angrily Thelma observed that only servants took Communion at noon and she supposed it was better to be damned than common.

For Thelma and me the wonder of Priscilla increased daily. Adolescence held no terrors for her. When we were gauche and fat or lean and gawky she became more rounded and graceful each term. Though our mothers spent pounds trying to make the school uniform of a brown dress and white collar (with cuffs to be put on for concerts and lectures) become us, we were always either drowned in it or oozing from it. Lady le Mesurier sent Priscilla back with butterflies embroidered on her collar. When I told my mother she sent me a set in Jap silk. It made no difference. I still looked an oaf and Priscilla a goddess. Matron's worst hair washing over a too-low basin and most agonising drying over an oil stove, which smelt, couldn't stop Priscilla's fair curls looking (as long ago her admirer from Derrington had said) like liquid sunshine. Mine hung dankly throughout the term and only recovered in the holidays when my mother had it cut almost as short as Ronald's and curled all over like the hair of my Early Victorian grandmother. Even Priscilla thought this was nice when we met in the holidays.

Swanage is not far from Broadstone and since my brother was at school at Derrington with her brother it was only natural we should come over. Meeting Priscilla in the holidays was even worse. She would wander round Swanage in the summer clad in simple summer frocks of pale blue check gingham and almost grown-up men would stop her and ask her to go to dances. She accepted only those whom her mother accepted for her. Nothing Priscilla ever did was ever outrée. Though spoiled by all she was never spoilt.

I would not wash up a tea cup, finding femininity an affront to my feminism. Priscilla would help the le Mesurier maids, not because they needed help, but because she must learn how in case she married a poor man. She was clever as well. Far cleverer than me. She passed the school certificate and won exemption for her matriculation at fifteen whereas Miss Fleming told my mother that I was useless for exams because I knew no arithmetic, geometry or algebra. What hurt most was that Priscilla's poetry did not make one blush like mine, but was accepted by *Nash's Magazine*.

Her brother Peter was a wonderful person too. Ronald and I agreed that the le Mesuriers were absolutely all right. Our enthusiasm for their household annoyed and mystified my mother. Was our house not larger? Was our food not nicer? Fair girls wore badly towards thirty. Ronald had beaten Peter in the 220. Lady le Mesurier might think herself very wonderful, but the title was only a knighthood and it was odd, say what she might, that her husband never came home on leave from foreign parts.

In fact Fort Ailsa was not a very remarkable house. It fronted on to the usual seaside road of the early 1900s and had a small garden and not much outlook. Our new house at Broadstone was far more imposing, having two acres of pine trees, a semi-circular drive, a billiard room and a view of the golf links. It also had a galleried staircase that my mother had painted scarlet, and a porch with Tudor beams which were mock only in period, being made of the finest timber. Brown Gates beat Ailsa Crag hollow and yet we revered Ailsa Crag. In it dance records were always playing, someone was always ringing the hairdressers, there was always a dance that night. It was the abode of a goddess. Visiting Ailsa Crag adolescence smote me so hard that when at lunch Lady le Mesurier asked me how old I was I could only say I didn't know. My embarrassment was doubled when after lunch Ronald swung a niblick in the absent Sir Hugh's study and was asked by the le Mesurier who was down from Oxford whether he was a Philistine.

Being with the le Mesuriers brought up the new problem of what we were going to do after we had finished being at school. I began to realise that I should not be at Fieldend forever. Already my brother had exchanged Derrington for Shrewsbury. Priscilla was to leave Fieldend at sixteen and spend a year in Paris. I thought this would be a good thing too, not because I had ever heard of Paris except as the capital of France, but because I should be with her. My mother thought the idea excellent since a finishing school would make me hold myself well and be feminine. My father agreed, but hoped it wouldn't give me expensive ideas. Lady le Mesurier gave my mother Madame's address and it was arranged that I should go in a year. Priscilla would go a term sooner, but then she was three months older. Since I didn't want to stay at Fieldend any longer I could go to Keswick to stay with my godmother and be taught literature and French by her sister. I grew up.

I wanted to grow up into a person, but not into a woman. Female prospects filled me with despair. I wasn't pretty like my mother, I couldn't put on clothes as she could, or arrange flowers or speak to servants. On the other hand I couldn't play games like my father and my brother and didn't really fit into their kind of male world. What would become of me? No one would marry me and since I could pass no examinations I couldn't even be a school mistress and blow whistles like Miss Smith. Just as I became desperate about myself I met a human being who found me an answer.

Her name was Mary Maud Chambers and she had scarlet bobbed hair and walked the streets of Bournemouth in a magenta cloak. I owed my acquaintance with her to my mother's insatiable quest for arts and crafts. We went into the shop she was serving in (it was the beginning of the craze for shops run by ladies) to see if we could find a barbola waste-paper basket. There were hundreds and while we were selecting one my mother noticed Mary Maud Chambers and asked her to tea. I cannot imagine what my mother saw in her since she didn't like golf or *thés dansants* or talk about people in the *Tatler* who she didn't know and my mother didn't know either. But I know what I saw in her. I saw an emancipated female human being.

Taking off her magenta cloak and combing her red curls in my bedroom she looked at the various prayers to St Teresa that decked the walls (my mother had liked their blue frames) and observed that she didn't believe in God. Shocked as never before I asked what did she live for. She replied, 'Knowledge.'

'Come along, you two,' called my mother and we went down to lunch. It hadn't been exactly a conversation, but it had changed my life. Soon the prayers to St Teresa were replaced on the wall by rhyme sheets from the Poetry Bookshop provided by Maud Mary. One was by Humbert Wolfe and said:

> 'What will they give me when journey's done?'
> 'Your own room to be quiet in, son.'

The other, more cheerful, and therefore for me less admirable, was about a blackbird and a star. People who didn't care for poetry in books let alone on walls would glance at them and look embarrassed. Inspired by Mary Maud I was beginning to like being different.

I never knew her at all well. I doubt if she noticed me at all. After a few months selling arts and crafts in Bournemouth she departed to run a poetry bookshop in Hull. Still, meeting her had answered my question. When I was old enough I should go away and earn my living in London.

I didn't mind now when coy Miss Lipton with her too-long nose and fluffy hair said there was no place in the world for clever women. Where had her silliness led her except to sit and fret while thirty girls ate spaghetti and tomato (called at Fieldend bloody worms) for supper? It wasn't much of a life and all those little pink jumpers she knitted couldn't hide the fact that she wasn't getting any younger. I despised her for the way she giggled when she spoke of Derrington masters. Even the Miss Flemings always declared they had had their chances when marriage was mentioned. Told to write an essay on 'The Ideal Woman' I endowed mine with wit, brains and an independent spirit. Priscilla's had courage and tenderness and won top marks.

Before she had left for Hull Mary Maud had given me her copy of *The Martyrdom of Man.* I read it every night under the bedclothes and each night tried harder not to say my prayers. Now that I was intellectually convinced there was no God I longed for him passionately. To comfort myself I wrote a manifesto declaring that it was better art for the greatest story in the world to end tragically (with the Crucifixion) than happily (with the Resurrection). I stopped myself praying in church with the sternness of a puritan forbidding himself the maypole. I wouldn't let my lips even move in the Creed.

When my mother announced I was leaving after the summer, Miss Fleming discovered an unexpected passion for me. If I stayed another year I might have been a prefect. I was becoming such a nice child. Now I had been a year in the top form didn't my mother think I ought to have a year of responsibility?

But in my mind I had already gone. Priscilla spoilt our last term by having appendicitis in the cottage hospital and coming back, charmingly pale, just in time to hear herself described as 'the ideal schoolgirl' at the prize giving. Six of us were leaving and either Miss Fleming had run out of epithets when she came to me or she could think of nothing polite to say, for she just said, 'And Helen, how long have you been with us, Helen?'

Being called an ideal schoolgirl made Priscilla weep a lot. Thelma and I comforted her, embarrassing her to the last by our unrestrained and emotional devotion. Perhaps she felt that she would never again be so happy and successful, whereas we felt that we could never again be so miserable or such failures.

Thelma was to go to a finishing school in Versailles. Both she and Priscilla were to have 'seasons'. I hugged my secret. By the time they were presented I should be riding in a bus to work, dressed from head to toe in orange handwovens.

I had begun to feel a great comfort in long-haired stuffs. When other girls pined for high heels I pined for the products of gentlewomen weavers. Lemon curdling to orange with a final tinge of purple had a special allure. Whereas in childhood I had pined in vain for a white fur coat I now thought it wicked to wear the skins of animals and winced at the poor faces of my mother's skunks.

Keswick was, in fact, a suitable place for me. It was as earnest as I was. There was at that time no cinema and the population amused itself with University Extension Lectures and League of Nations Union meetings. A dance mistress came every Tuesday from Carlisle especially to teach me and it seemed as though I Fox-Trotted in the ballroom of the local hotel with a denizen of Gomorrah.

My godmother lived with her elder sister Greta in an eighteenth-century terrace house near the bridge over the river Greta. The sisters, like their house and like the river, were part of Keswick. I didn't know anything of the beauty of eighteenth-century terrace houses then and their house seemed to me thin and meagre. Even to me its garden was lovely, however. It had a mulberry tree and a stone wall separated it from meadows. Wherever I looked I could see mountains. My godmother and her sister found them beautiful, but I thought that they shut me away from the Paris where wanted to be with Priscilla.

The English Lakes in autumn have a melancholy beauty. I suppose one can feel very old or very young in adolescence. At sixteen I felt very old. I had come to the end of the only life I knew about. I was infinitely disillusioned. When my godmother insisted that I accompanied her to church I went with her in pity. I found it touching that she and her sister had reached fifty and still believed in God. Their goodness seemed to me to make them very young.

Greta (who wasn't my godmother but who taught me) had white hair done back in a bun and eyes the colour of the river she was called after. Kitty (my godmother) had red hair that was greying and eyes bright as a fox's. Greta liked to stay at home and read or play the piano, but Kitty liked to be high up the mountains. Every ledge of Skiddaw was friendly to her. She wore breeches with holes in them that were part of history and when she went up the road to do the shopping her eyes were always on the hills.

They took me long bicycle rides that tired me far more than they tired them and we paused at the top of every hill to appreciate the views. I shall always associate with these expeditions my total failure to respond to natural beauty. Scenes that had inspired Wordsworth and Shelley merely made me pray that when we pedalled home I'd find a letter from Paris from Priscilla. The mountains were my gaolers, the lakes reminded me in vain of my beloved sea.

I don't suppose my godmother and her sister entertained happy memories of an adolescent who stole all their bullseyes (how hungry my woes made me!) and slept through those musical Wednesdays when neighbours dropped in to play Bach on violin and cello while Greta accompanied them on the piano.

Sometimes neighbours would put chains on their cars and drive us across the snowy passes to Windermere or Grasmere to hear concerts of chamber music given by famous quartets. I enjoyed these, not for the music, since I was and am tone deaf, but for the pleasure of sitting in the back of the car and dreaming. How many entirely happy lives have I lived in the back of cars!

Kitty and Greta had friends called the Halls who lived in a large house over the river and would often ask me in to play bridge after dinner. I couldn't play and their offer to teach me was thought ill of by my godmother who didn't think bridge a very commendable accomplishment. Their son would try to kiss me on the way home. It didn't give me any pleasure, but I liked him trying because it gave me status. I felt that like the bridge and my dancing lessons kissing made me worldly. I even allowed the young man (he was perhaps twenty-eight) to take me to tennis tournaments. My tennis was deplorable and I despised athleticism, but going there in his sports car was satisfactorily wicked.

I wanted Kitty and Greta's disapproval then as much as I should relish their approval now. When one is young it is pleasant to shock people of integrity.

I did not realise how much I liked the house by the bridge until my mother arrived with Babs and announced her intention of taking me away from it. They were on a motor tour and would 'do' the Lakes and then return home via Shrewsbury so as to see Ronald. According to my mother Kitty and Greta were dear things but terrible old maids. She pooh-poohed the schemes Greta had for me which centred round

Oxford.

'Don't be so silly. Of course my Helen will marry.' I hadn't thought Greta had thought much of me, but when she told my mother that our reading had given her rare pleasure I felt ashamed. My mother was confident that our car bore me off to a better world, but now when I have letters from Keswick I wonder.

My list of clothes for Paris said three evening dresses. Hitherto I had only had one and that an affair of taffeta and tulle. My mother took me to a tiny shop in Bournemouth with a disconcertingly simple name and put me in the hands of its owner, who said that I was not exactly pretty, but had charm, which was much nicer. Looking back on her judgment I think it charitable. The more they tried on dresses, taking them off again and observing that they were not me, the more certain I became that there wasn't any me at all, that the existence of this girl Helen Fletcher who was being fitted out to go to Paris was an illusion.

Oddly enough, though I can remember few of my past dresses I can remember the three evening dresses I took to Paris quite well. They all had no sleeves and a waist round the thighs. One was yellow merging to orange like a sunset or a poached egg and trimmed with orange beads. One was powder blue and trimmed with feathers. One was green and could be worn for a garden party or reception with a hat made by Ida Mann for that purpose. They were all short. I suppose that a girl with the figure of a nymph and the poise of a goddess could have looked nice in them. I couldn't. It was a trying period to grow up in.

I was to go out into the great world. My father had had a talk to my brother when he went out into it at Shrewsbury and now perhaps my mother should have had a talk to me. Probably she meant to one of those mornings driving back from fittings at the dress shop, but something always stopped her. She was not even prompted when I came out of a telephone box and told her that a man with a white beard had offered to give me a pair of Russian boots. Perhaps she thought that a girl who knew so much of *The Green Hat* by heart knew what it was about. I didn't and my ignorance passed for sophistication.

On my last night in England we went to see the play *The Green Hat*. My father and brother were at home at Broadstone and I persuaded my mother to take a box. I had been to the London theatre twice, once to see *Chu Chin Chow* and once to a farce called *Oh Julie*. *The Green Hat* was different. Everyone spoke in tense, drawling voices and had white haggard faces. Tallulah Bankhead kept asserting that her lover had an illness which made my mother shudder. Since I had no notion what the play was about I suffered no moral harm. Tallulah Bankhead (or just Tallulah as my finishing school soon taught me to call her) seemed innocent and beautiful as Titania. I secreted her picture from the programme and slept with it underneath my pillow.

– 11 –

My mother need not have worried about recognising Madame at Victoria. There she was in black satin with a heaving bosom, awaiting her pupils at the barrier. She gave me a look that seemed to take in my brown handwoven coat in all its hairiness and observed that evidently this was another type than Priscilla. Or rather that was what I took her French to mean. I don't know what my mother thought it meant, but she gave Gwen, in whose house we had been staying, one of those looks and Gwen said, 'Well, we'd best be getting along, Helen. I want to take your mother shopping before she goes back to Ronald.'

Before I could stop them they had deserted me. I stood beside Madame while she greeted the exquisite daughter of a Harley Street specialist and her scarcely more elegant mother. (How long, I wondered, did it take for Madame to make one look as grand as that?) I prayed that there might be other new girls. There were. They came up the platform just as Madame had begun to worry about missing the train. I felt it was a good thing that my mother had gone because she wouldn't have approved of them or their mothers. They were exactly alike and dressed in pearl chokers and coats with fur collars. Their mothers were exactly alike and dressed in fur coats and ropes of pearls. All were short and fat and all had enormous noses. Madame called one girl Rachel and the other Rebecca. I thought it was clever of her to know which was which.

Although she had eight girls that time including me, that would be all for the journey because the others had been to Chamonix for the Christmas holidays and were waiting for us in Paris. The doctor's daughter asked if they had had a good time and Madame launched into an account of the success Priscilla and another girl called Tania had had with 'jeunes gens'. I asked her what these were and she told me 'young men'.

It was embarrassing that she could say things to the doctor's daughter about one and one's French wouldn't quite stretch to them. Patting my knees she observed, 'Hélène sait qu'elle a des beaux jambes.'

When Audrey told me what this meant I felt as angry as if to have beautiful legs were an insult. I tried to pull my skirts down.

On the boat Madame made a sailor find us deck chairs and sent for champagne. I had never had this before except at Christmas, but she said it was good for sea sickness. We drank it and ate apples, but this didn't stop Rebecca and Rachel turning dark green and rushing to the railings.

Muttering something about 'Pas comme il faut' Madame manoeuvred them below. With the insensitivity of the non-seasick I wondered why if one were naturally yellow and knew one would turn green when seasick one should choose a dark green coat like Rebecca. On the other hand Rachel's wine-coloured one looked almost worse. From the friendly way Madame talked in English about my home and father and brother once she had settled them with the stewardess I guessed they had made a very bad impression and unwittingly done me a good turn.

I had never been abroad before and now I saw it not with the seeing eye of childhood, but with the blind eye of adolescence. It would be years before I saw anything unconnected with me. If I saw at all it was with words and in the clanging train between Calais and Paris I murmured to myself about 'the vasty fields of France'. They looked a little like the downs around Salisbury but barer and bigger. Not like abroad at all. The part of me that had expected a carpet down Ludgate Hill would not have been surprised had French grass been red or puce.

Madame had lost her money when the Germans took Alsace and keeping a finishing school seemed very dreadful to her. To alleviate her lot she charged the highest prices (£80 for a nine-week term and approximately as much again for extras) and interrupted her own life as little as possible. To procure herself champagne she bought us champagne. Lunch on the train seemed to a schoolgirl the epitome of elegance. I had never had champagne twice in one day and I felt hot and dizzy. The lunch car seemed to turn upside down and wherever I looked I saw Madame's huge white face with lettuce sticking out of the mouth in all directions. She ate it, as I was to learn later, in the same manner and quantity as a rabbit. It was no embarrassment to her to have a piece half in and half out in the midst of conversation. With black coffee (which I loathed) there was Benedictine that tasted like honey and pepper. I longed for a glass of water, but was too frightened to ask for it.

Priscilla would be waiting in the school in Paris. I had made a calendar in Keswick which counted the hours till I saw her. Now I didn't want to. I felt so far away from my Fieldend self that the thought of seeing someone who had known me there was frightening. Besides I had perfected a way of living as though I were in a comfortable glass coffin. So long as I lay still in it nothing could hurt me. I could see people but they could not see me, or anyway not the real me. I felt afraid that Priscilla would spoil all this.

Madame's flat was in the Rue George Berger, a few yards from Parc Monceau. It was not like a London flat at all. When you had walked past the bedroom of a cross old woman called the concierge who could always see you when you didn't think she was looking because of concealed mirrors (could she really see us or was this part of Madame's subtle discipline?) you went in a creaking lift to the first floor where a huge mahogany door was opened by a savage-looking maid called Hortense. The hall was huge and slippery and there was nothing in it except a gilt table with a marble top and three legs. All the doors leading out of it were made of glass so that you could see through them. Privacy was further infringed by white plaster cupids who peered from the ceilings. Where two rooms had been made out of one (to turn the flat into a school) one bedroom would have a cupid's bottom and another its face.

Priscilla and three other girls waited in the hall. Madame kissed them all passionately, which made it seem inadequate when Priscilla and I said 'Hello'. It was months since we had seen each other and she had seen them yesterday.

Priscilla still looked quite human in spite of her being half finished. She wore a printed crêpe-de-chine frock with daisies on it. With her was Kate, a tall fair creature who was clearly quite grown-up (I learnt later she was an orphaned heiress whom Madam found it profitable to chaperone). If grown-ups could be human she was. Then there was Mary who was fat and wore the kind of dark green dress worn by my Salisbury cousins. She looked as frightened as I felt (I discovered afterwards that she had not been in Chamonix, but had been delivered that afternoon by her parents direct to the school). Finally there was the most inhuman and terrifying girl I had ever seen. Her name was Tania and she wore a magenta dress and had red hair. If anyone else had done this you would have thought they might not have known it clashed. One look at Tania and you knew that if it did she meant it to, that clashes were the thing this year. She was the most elegant and finished creature I had ever seen. I thought she must be twenty at least.

At dinner I learnt that she was sixteen, a month younger than I was and the school baby. I felt that perhaps she had been born finished. She had small amber eyes and a way of looking at you as though she saw you had torn underclothes. She spoke with a voice that expired at the end of each sentence. You felt she was bored and tired and that politeness cost her a lot. The only person she was nice to (other than Madame whom she treated as an equal) was Priscilla. I could see that Priscilla liked her very much.

For dinner we had soup made of lots of small pieces of vegetables and called by Madame complexion broth, a salad made of something prickly and covered with oil (I hated this and Madame said I would be let off as it was my first dinner, but I must always eat it afterwards because like the broth it was good for my complexion), roast chicken without any bread sauce and spinach made into a cream served by itself. Finally there was white ice cream with hot chocolate sauce. Though odd like everything else this was nice. There was white wine and Madame told me to drink mine up because I was in France now.

After dinner we went into a small room called the salon. It had the same polished floor and there was very little in it except gilt chairs and sofas covered in dark red and a piano. Tania played a tune called *Madelon*. Mary began to cry and I fell asleep only to be shaken awake and told to go to bed.

Tania slept with Priscilla and I was to sleep with Mary. There were two beds in each room. I thought I would never sleep because she wept and called on the Virgin Mary (she was a Catholic from Lincolnshire and had never before left her horses) and outside carts clattered over the cobbles. But I was tired and the next thing I knew was that Madame was bending over me in her dressing-gown and telling me to wash my face and put on my dressing-gown and come to petit déjeuner. When she had told me this she kissed both my cheeks. This was the traditional method of waking at her pension.

As well as sharing a bedroom Mary and I shared a tiny place called a cabinet de toilette where we could wash and keep our tooth brushes. I washed my face and combed my hair and went into the room where we had had dinner.

It was clear that my dressing-gown was quite wrong. Nothing in the list had prepared my mother for this breakfast business and she had bought me a nice plain warm dressing-gown of camel hair. Everyone else round the table had flowing gowns of satin and silk and velvet. Only Mary, who came in red-eyed and late, had one like mine. But it wasn't only my dressing-gown. Madame was shocked at my face. Where were my manners that I expected to breakfast with her and with my fellow pupils without lipstick or powder? Was this how nice girls (she called them jeunes filles bien-élevées) behaved in Salisbury?

'But I haven't got any lipstick.'

'Then go and powder your face, Hélène.'

When I returned she said how odd it was that the English never powdered anything but the nose. That was all that she said about me because Mary had created a diversion by saying that she thought it wicked to use lipstick or face powder, and Madame was having as much fun with her little barbarian from the wilds of England, as she called Mary, as keepers have with tame bears.

Oddly enough it was Tania who stopped her by saying must she have all her meals disturbed with tears and couldn't Madame do her training away from the table.

'You know, Madame darling, I always wake up with a headache. It's sheer cruelty to wake us up so dreadfully early.'

It was nine o'clock.

After breakfast, which consisted of two small pieces of bread, a tiny piece of butter and a teaspoonful of honey, plus a large cup of coffee with skin floating in it, and which I knew I should find no difficulty in remembering to call petit déjeuner, we were told to make our beds and put out our clothes so that Madame could inspect them. The heels of my day shoes were too low, but otherwise I was all right. Mary had everything wrong and was made to compile a list to send to her mother in Lincolnshire. Madame herself would supervise the buying of the new wardrobe in

Paris. This would be fun for us all as it would mean going to some dress shows. As for me my shoes would be bought that afternoon at Pinets.

After our wardrobes had been inspected and put away Madame took Mary and me into a small inky room where the others were studying with a lady called Madame de l'Etoile. The prospectus of the school had mentioned that among the subjects studied were Philosophy, French Literature and Anecdotal History. (This last, I learnt as time went by, meant the lives of the French Kings' mistresses.) Whatever they were doing when we came in was stopped and Mary and I were given a lesson on accent while the others listened and giggled. Mary had a good working knowledge of French and no accent and I had no accent and no working knowledge. (Miss Smith had not known enough to impart any with certainty and we had always tortured Fieldend mademoiselles.) Our efforts to pronounce lists of words ending in -eux and -ieux were funny.

The salle d'étude was next door to Madame's linen cupboard. I was soon to learn that everything we said she heard. She came in now and, hearing the others laughing at us, said, 'Elles sont terribles, n'est ce pas, mais les autres sont pires?' This made everyone laugh and seeing me bewildered Tania said in a whisper, 'She says you are awful but not so awful as the others.'

Until then I had forgotten Rachel and Rebecca. They had not put in an appearance at dinner or petit déjeuner. Now they came in smiling and were introduced to Madame de l'Etoile. I noticed that they were not so awed by her as they were by Madame, perhaps because she spoke gently and looked poor.

When lunch (or déjeuner) started it was plain that

the term had started. We spoke French or did not speak at all and we ate what was handed to us. The prickly salad appeared again and I managed to swallow a little. When I thought my troubles were over the maid handed some delicious creamy ice cream. I let myself go with it and was horrified to find it was sour and not sweet although sugar was handed with it. Madame kept everyone else round the table an extra five minutes while I finished my petit suisse.

That afternoon Madame felt too fatigued to take us to Pinet's and so Madame de l'Etoile took us to the Louvre. I hoped it would mean that I should 'walk with' Priscilla, but at our pension you did not really walk with anyone. Taxis were put down on the bill and you then took trams or the metro unless some rich person like Kate or Tania volunteered to pay for the taxi.

Almost every finishing school in Paris was 'doing' the Louvre and almost every unattended young Frenchman seemed to be watching them do it. Madame de l'Etoile's progress through the galleries of Primitives was deflected by a young man in a beret who tried to pass a note to Priscilla. Her appeals to Tania and Priscilla, and in a minor key to Audrey, the specialist's daughter, to behave like nice well-bred young ladies were useless. No one looked at the pictures of toy Christs dying. I didn't either. His agony seemed to me no greater than my agony when I watched Priscilla laughing at the private jokes of Tania.

We had to go home early because that night we were to go to a Cours du Dance. From the tenor of Madame's remarks about our hair and complexions at tea I gathered that this was to my finishing school what a netball match had been to Fieldend. All the pensions in Paris came to it and we were on our honour to look our prettiest for the sake of the school.

Mary had been weeping on and off all day and it was decided at tea (if you could call it that) that she had better stay at home and go to bed early. I knew this was really because she had only a white dress she had worn at Roedean to be confirmed in. Madame could not leave her other three new girls at home and parade her success as a pension keeper to her fellow madames. I was commanded to wear my yellow (the one that looked like a poached egg or a sunset) and Rebecca and Rachel were suitably instructed. Madame herself came in and brushed my hair and put pink powder on my cheeks with her own puff and lipstick on my lips with a lipstick she left with me.

When we were ready we gathered in the hall and were made to walk up and down under the bright lights. Priscilla in white looked like an angel. Tania in black looked like a wicked lady. Kate dressed in sequins seemed somehow non-competitive, adult and reassuring. When we reached Monsieur Raymond's terrifying mirrored salon she took me with her to the ladies' cloakroom. She had powder in a small gilt box and she lent it to me. We went into the ballroom together.

It was the etiquette of these occasions to put all the jeunes filles along one wall and all the jeunes gens along the other. It was not hard to find Madame because (as she had boasted) her pension was by far the prettiest. Even if her new girls let her down she had Tania and Priscilla, and Audrey looked at least a lady. Besides there was Kate who looked herself and a grown-up.

Behaviour was simple. You sat in a row beside Madame until a man came over and asked you to dance. All dances danced scored to your side; all dances sat out scored against you.

The French girls were easy to recognise because they wore two lots of long hair. That on their heads curled and frizzed and that beneath their arms did likewise. The French Priscilla (or was it the French Tania?) had long bushes underneath her arms that you could have plaited. I found this as shocking as I later found the women breast-feeding their babies or their employers' babies on the benches in Parc Monceau.

Monsieur Raymond clearly thought a lot of our pension because he came at once and asked me to dance. Or perhaps he did not quite ask me but demanded a new girl of Madame who persisted in regarding me as a lesser evil than the two she now referred to as 'nos Israelites'. I took long English steps and he took short French steps and when I had fallen over his small dancing master's feet forty times he told Madame that I had no grace and was in need of private dancing lessons.

My evening would have been a total loss, but for an elderly gentleman who everyone referred to as 'le comte' asking me to tango. He threw me here, he threw me there, and though insensible I was apparently commendable. Anyway he came back for me again and again and Madame teased me about my 'vieux chevalier'. I should have been happier about my conquest if out of the corner of my eye I did not see Tania and Priscilla who persisted in breaking the unwritten law and dancing a waltz together before the jeunes gens had time to grab them. They looked very cool and composed and at home. I loathed Tania.

When we arrived home we went into the huge kitchen and Madame heated huge bars of chocolate from a shop called Felix Potin and we drank it with cream and crisp croissants which we dipped in. I tried to say goodnight to Priscilla as we went down the passage to our bedrooms, but Tania said mockingly, 'Tell me darling, is this the broken-hearted swain whose letters you used to read in the lavatory?' I fled to unite my tears with those of Mary.

Next day was Sunday and Madame announced at petit déjeuner that we should all go to the Embassy church. Mary protested that she was a Catholic and Madame said so was she, but she went to church with us and so could Mary. But this was too much. Mary would not. Never would she enter a building so unhallowed. She would powder her face, wear sleeveless dresses, anything. But she would not enter a Protestant church. Clearly even Madame thought she had gone too far for she sent Hortense to fetch Madame de l'Etoile to conduct Mary to the Madeleine.

'But you, Madame, are a Catholic.'

'Mais oui, ma cherie, mais pas pratiquante.'

It was rather nice at the Embassy church because one felt in England. The hymns and psalms and service were exactly as they were at home. And there, for all to gaze at, was the Ambassador. I can't say I felt religious but I felt patriotic. I hoped my conscience would not make me refuse to go on grounds of agnosticism. To appease it I was careful not to shut my eyes to pray and to leave the Creed unsaid.

Outside the church surprisingly there was Thelma. France seemed to have claimed her completely for she came up and kissed Priscilla and me on both cheeks.

There in one small street was assembled the finishing school population of Paris. In the five minutes' conversation permitted by our respective madames we learnt that Thelma fenced while we didn't, but that our school was the only one that permitted déjeuner en peignoir. Thelma's was larger too. Almost as big as Fieldend. The knowledge that she and the thousand or so other finishing-school pupils envied us made us see Madame's establishment in a different light. Perhaps after all we were fortunate and sophisticated.

AFTERWORD

INTRODUCTION 1947

When and why did Helen Fletcher give to her autobiography the title *A Gay Goodnight*? It is her own title, a characteristic choice, with its mingled lightness and regret. Her sudden death in September 1947 has invested it with a tragic aptitude.

Although Helen Fletcher had begun work on her autobiography at least four years earlier, it was unfinished when she died. Her work as a film critic for *Time and Tide*, the *Sunday Graphic* and the BBC took up most of her time, for she was conscientious and, like most good writers, she achieved her effect of delighted and delightful fluency only through hours of hard work at her desk. Moreover she had too well-balanced a view of life and set too high a value on the art of living to immure herself writing of the past instead of going out to live in the present. And so the autobiography was never completed.

She has told her own story only as far as her eighteenth year. She observed her surroundings, even as a child, with an acute and critical eye, and her account, vivid in detail and often rich in incident, is edged with wit; but this is not the story of a happy childhood. Childhood is rarely a happy time for the clever and sensitive; even the wisest treatment cannot prevent the frustration which arises when the child's sensibility and ambition beat wretchedly against the limitations of its age. Or the anguish of having poetry as good as Shakespeare's inchoate in the head, while all that the fat hand and blunt pencil can produce is a patently inferior quatrain. . . . Helen had other troubles besides those which must in any case have been hers. Her education did nothing to increase her self-confidence, so that it took her in after life many years to recognise her ability and to learn to trust herself to it. There were gropings towards a writer's career, occasional articles, occasional reviews, a short story. More often than not these fragments remained unfinished, or were put away and forgotten. She wrote with extreme difficulty and a self-criticism which prevented her from ever regarding anything as finished: it was never good enough to please her. Only, perhaps, through the relentless compulsion of journalism could her talent be brought to bear fruit.

In the spring of 1944 Lady Rhondda, who had long believed in her ability, asked her to become film critic on *Time and Tide*. Helen, after expressing some misgivings as to whether copy would ever arrive before press-day, agreed to try. From that day until the Monday before her death, she produced her article with automatic regularity. What midnight watches and last-minute anxieties went before it were, so to speak, none of our business. But on Monday morning, rain or fine, sun or snow, good programmes or bad, there was Helen's article. Journalism, because of this regularity, may become a soul-destroying occupation. I do not think it was so for Helen, because what she had needed above all was some outside dispassionate force to cut short her self-criticism and hesitation and compel her to write 'finis' and send the article to the printer.

Working this weekly treadmill she not only established herself with astonishing rapidity at the top of her profession as a critic, but began rapidly to develop as a writer. She gained fluency and assurance and a just view of her own abilities. The tragedy was that she did not live long enough for her new-found confidence to bear fruit, except in her critical articles themselves and in the pages of the autobiography on which she worked in her spare time.

It is difficult to write about Helen, because it is impossible to think of her in such *in memoriam* terms as this kind of introduction usually seems to call for. Her vitality was what mattered, the eagerness of her intrest, the sharpness of her critical sense, the vibrating liveliness of her mind. She should have died hereafter when life, with its changing *tempi*, its intervals of leisure, its alternating stretches of activity and repose, had given her the opportunity to write as well as to live. So much had begun to appear in her mind as success brought her talent to maturity and discovered new talents in her. Yet there is no wasted time to regret. Helen lived eagerly and fully. She loved and hated well. She suffered to the full the anguish and drank deep of the hope of her troubled, idealist, passionate and honest inter-war generation. She had cared for politics and for people, striven and suffered for individuals and for causes. She had married and had two sons of whom she was justly proud. She had known, with a full measure of the unhappiness which is the lot of humankind, also the transcendant happiness of a sustained and mutual attachment such as falls to few. Hers was a rich life, too rich in itself to leave her time for the recollecting and considering part and its later harvest.

Her autobiography, incomplete as it is, may well take its place as a minor masterpiece of this intimate art. For she was an artist, in her writing, in her perceptions, in her life.

C.V. Wedgwood